Putin's Praetorians

Confessions of the
Top Kremlin Trolls

Phil Butler

The author and publishers wish to thank the following for permission to use copyright material: Pepe Escobar, The Saker, Charles Bausman, Marcel Sardo, Patrick Armstrong, Graham Phillips, Malinka1102, Eric C. Anderson, Marilyn Justice, Holger Eekhof, Jeff Silverman, Chris Doyle, James Beagan, Carmen Renieri, Vanessa Beeley, Levent Alver, Vera van Horne, Christoph Heer, John Delacour, Greg Galloway, Tatiana Pahlen, Enrico Ivanov, Maria Engström, Dimitry Zolotarev, Paul Payer, Vladimir Samarin, Stanislav Stankevich, Margarita Simonyan

Cover Design and Illustrations: M.P.K Revita

ISBN-13: 978-3-9818919-0-4

DEDICATION

To my father Albert E. Butler, an American lawyer who believed in the pursuit of the truth and nothing but the truth. I would also like to dedicate my efforts to seek the facts of the matter of Russia's intentions, to my wife and partner Mihaela Lica Butler, without whose intuition and loyalty to principle I could never have approached the underlying actuality.

"The world has no room for cowards."
Robert Louis Stevenson

Table of Contents

Foreword

For many years in Germany I spent each morning strolling past the gray and weary figures of villagers. It was during those years, I become numbed to the realization they knew so little of the fate of our world. Every time I would enter the corner bakery I would see the same German celebrities staring up from the counter tabloids with clueless fake smiles. And while I waited for my coffee and bread pastry, I was often greeted by the austere face of Chancellor Angela Merkel with that same blank stare, looking up as if to ask, "And?"

Now we live in Greece, and there are times I stop to ponder how I got involved in all the geopolitical mumbo-jumbo that ensnares our world these days. I sometimes ask myself, "Just what kind of madness is it, after all, that propels average cattle to 'moo' a different tune than their bovine brethren?" As I write these words it is a happy circumstance that I am not alone in my unique mental clarity. The reasoning, it occurred to me, may just be the way to seek a better understanding between people and their ideals. The reason for this book then, it is to moderate relative truths. By showing you the sincerity and vigor with which a small group defends the other side of the story, perhaps me and my comrades can achieve the ultimate good.

So, the book you are reading is all about a relatively small group of ordinary people, everyday individuals who decided not to be cattle after all. The confessions you are about to read are telling.

As for my own motivations for becoming a Kremlin Troll, most people will identify these quite easily. Not a day goes by in which I fail to remember the name calling from the grammar school playground. Sharp mental images of the jabbing and finger pointing are burned into my brain. Those bullies and curmudgeons that would "one-up" us all, they lurk at the edges of my memory. Oh, how the decent among us grew to hate them, the bullies of the world that is. How could any of us have known back then that our country would become the bully of the world? Presidents and senators utter the cliché "This is not who we are", in order to suit their purposes. But as a common man I tell you, the world's bully is not what we were meant to become.

So, I thank God for our teachers and coaches back then. For without them no sliver of correctness or liberty would be remembered today. This is all I can say about being American. As for the deep-seated anger many feel, such meanness still stirs in me a poignant reminder of those lessons of right and wrong we learned back then. Writing this foreword, I remember the face and the words of the first indoctrinator of my own character, a physical education coach whose name I cannot recall. The lessons he meted out, the crisp justice all my athletic coaches exacted in all those rough games of my youth, I am thankful for being introduced to the etiquette of pain. Whatever the reasons for my taking up sport, I know we were all lucky in the fraternity of corporal logic. The swift suffering of fools and young psychopaths brings a smile these days, and the kinship many of us feel with Vladimir Putin rises from this.

These recollections point me to a better understanding for why some are fighting the meanness of today's false narratives. After all, isn't knowing right from wrong and trying to do the right thing what we were taught? Isn't this why we cheer and weep at the same movie moments? We do read and watch the same dramas repeatedly, don't we? Don't we all despise the same villains and adore the same heroes? It is these fundamental questions and the ideals behind that drive me. Whatever the reasons for our dedication to Putin, the thread of commonality you will find herein is clear as shimmering gold, and as sure as titanium. Good people despise bullies and cheats, and the people profiled in this book are all, finally pissed off.

The testimonies herein attest to the moral outrage that has surfaced. Many dissident voices have become disenchanted like me. You might be among those who are disappointed and angry too, for all I know. However, I am sure that leaders like Vladimir Putin gain their most loyal and ardent following from such disenfranchised people. The *Kremlin Trolls,* as we are sometimes called, are mutineers on the Orwellian ship of humanity. We inhabit social media of their own accord. And many of us risk much in raising our voices in protest of the false narrative. I know you will find these dissenters are entirely authentic, interesting and ultimately compelling too.

In the following confessions, I believe you'll find a dynamic variety of personalities with powerful voices. It is my hope, that this idealism and courage will make more voices rise above the empty nihilism and false narratives of our greatest enemies, the globalists. The world is in great peril. Hopefully, by the time you reach the end of the book, you will know the whole truth. For the revelations here are straight from the most important political voices of our time. While this is a bold claim, it is true, I assure you. And if you care enough to read until the end, then you will find out for yourself, the enemy of the world is an old one. The ruination of peace and harmony is not Vladimir Vladimirovich Putin. The great spoiler is the deceiver of antiquity brought forward. I pray that the testament of these honest people will open a window of truth for you. You have my best wishes regardless, and my thanks for your courage to take the tentative first steps away from the mindless herd.

"Which would you choose if you could:
pleasure for yourself despite your friends
or a share in their grief?"
Sophocles, *Ajax*

Introduction by Pepe Escobar

I've never suffered fools/simpletons/sub-zoology specimens gladly – or otherwise. When you've been around as a foreign correspondent for over three decades – all over the world – you think you've been through every swamp in the book. Oh no, you haven't seen the hysterical swamp accusing you 24/7 of being a Putin agent. So, here's me, on the record.

I was a Putin agent before I turned 15 when I read *Crime and Punishment* and *The Brothers Karamazov.* I was a Putin agent before studying the USSR in depth in college. I've been a Putin agent since before I marveled at the Paris-Moscow retrospective at the Beaubourg. I was even a Putin agent before I visited the USSR still in the Gorbachev era. I was a Putin agent before I arrived in Moscow on the Trans-Siberian just to check, live, in the Winter of 1992, that the Soviet Union was no more. I've been a Putin agent since before I covered drunken Yeltsin barely kept on his feet by Bubba Clinton at the Kremlin. I was a Putin agent long before the ruble crisis of 1998 when I was commuting between the Caucasus, Central Asia, and Moscow. I was a Putin agent before covering Putin's election in 2000 and partying hard at the Metropol every night. I was a Putin agent before I was invited by RT to be a guest on camera and to write Op-Eds. I was a Putin agent before I signed a contract with Sputnik as a columnist. I've been a Putin agent since decades before Oliver Stone told me in a dinner he was editing a Putin documentary. I've been a Putin agent since before Russia itself formed out of the permafrost. And yes, I'll remain a Putin agent even after I return to dust.

Now piss off.

Pepe Escobar, Asia Times

Chapter I: My Kremlin Bona Fides

*"My notion of the KGB came from romantic spy
stories. I was a pure and utterly successful
product of Soviet patriotic education."
-- Vladimir Putin*

You've probably picked up this book because of the provocative title. Maybe the challenging nature of it spoke to something in you. Or as we say in the business of PR, the title "resonated" with you. One way or another, you are reading what I am writing because you cannot help but want the truth about Russia, the Kremlin, and the new crises. Maybe you want to know more about Vladimir Putin? It could be you need to know for sure if he is just "that" evil. Or if he is just "that" good. You ultimately chose to read this book to help make a bit more sense of an insane world we all live in. As it turns out, we have a lot in common. Our "commonality" is one reason I decided to disclose my real role in working for the Kremlin. Or for the Russians. Or for the truth about Russia. What and who I am working for will become apparent pretty soon. Loyalties aside, my life has led me into contact with people you may have read about, the "Kremlin Trolls", that army of disruptors who we were told were paid to disrupt democratic societies. What you are about to read is my story, their story, and the story of one of the most remarkable political movements in today's world. Most reading here will be surprised at what is really going on behind the scenes in this new Cold War. Meanwhile, others among you might feel as vindicated as I, for a genuine effort in supporting the truth.

The cognitive dissonance I am talking about reminds me of something from the Hollywood film *A Few Good Men*. In the movie, actor Jack Nicholson delivers a memorable and forceful outburst on the witness stand in a military tribunal. In this scene Nicholson, who plays the role of US Marine Colonel Nathan Jessup, undergoes an aggressive cross examination. Fellow actor Tom Cruise, as US Navy JAG lawyer, Lieutenant Kaffe, grills the tough Marine colonel. At the end of Cruise's (Lieutenant Kaffe's) gripping questioning, Nicholson (Colonel Jessup) breaks down and bellows: "You want the truth? You can't handle the truth." Every time I watch the movie I'm still riveted at the significance of the moment. This reply to the JAG attorney's badgering is telling, riveting, and indicative of our society's obtuseness these days. The scene reveals in an instant our unwillingness to face reality. The moment in the film is iconic because it lays bare the mental disconnect truth sometimes forces us to suffer. Now the truth is often obscured for this very reason: it's just too damned hard to admit.

Now, I hope every reader here can imagine my sudden dismay in realizing that my countrymen are no longer wearing the white hats these days. If you can accept that I am a veteran and a patriot, then you can imagine my surprise at becoming a Putin fanboy too. What's more, try to visualize my own ideological deconstruction after half a century of programming, and the people I am about to introduce you to are better understood. As shocked as my old friends were shocked to see me in TV interviews on Russian media, most are now in utter dismay over subsequent world events. But before I get ahead of myself here, let me transport you back to the start. Let me show you Phil Butler the journalist back before I put myself in such a controversial position. It's important for you to know my motivations for joining Vladimir Putin's side in the information war, to grasp the cool reality of this new Cold War.

The first time I mentioned Vladimir Putin in one of my articles was via our Argophilia Travel News from back in October of 2010. It was then, that Prime Minister Vladimir Putin was often mentioned in connection with Russia's pursuit of closer ties with Europe and the EU. The article I recall was about tourism and free visa regimes Russia sought with the EU. It was a travel report entitled "To Russia With Love", a story about Mr. Putin coming back from Zurich and Russia's bid for the 2018 FIFA World Cup. At the time, my tone toward Putin and Russia was positive-neutral. This was owing to my wife's being Romanian, and because Argophilia was positioned to tell about Eastern European travel news. Subsequent stories relayed the ongoing news of the time. But an interview later that year with the folks at Welcome to Russia, amplified the Russian government's efforts to ramp up the country's tourism. These events were a catalytic variable for me, and it was not long afterward Europe benefited from a massive influx of Russian travelers. So, the stage was set, as I later reported, for a visa-free regime to and from Russia. Underneath the tourism news though, there was an unseen, by me and many others, underpinning to the stories. You may recall that back in 2011, Russian Prime Minister Vladimir Putin was in the mix of Russian presidential candidates once again. During this time, he was also pleading with the EU for the aforementioned visa regimen. The regimen Putin sought would have propelled EU-Russia relations to the next positive level. Another story I wrote for Argophilia reflected the nearly desperate positivity Putin and Russia leveled at Brussels and EU nations. Ironically, my story also mentioned an initiative we would later see taking hold. If I may quote myself here, maybe the reader will be fascinated to discover the first translucent glimpse of a Kremlin Troll in the making. This is from Argophilia Travel News on October 5th of 2011:

> *"With the Russian Federation literally begging the EU to normalize visa restrictions the last couple of years, and Putin being continually stone walled by the EU's core constituents, it's no small wonder Russia's most influential leader turned to new strategies. Whether or not his brandishing of this new plan is grandstanding or not? Well, Putin is not exactly known for bluffing."*

Another interesting footnote became visible searching Argo News' archives for references to Putin. I mentioned my wife's influence in suggesting I study more closely Putin and Russia. So, I became all the more fascinated with her input when I ran across a body language article she wrote about Putin's so-called "gunslinger" arm- swing. I took note of the fact her assessment was some years before Western mainstream media proclaimed he had Alzheimer's disease. A body language expert since her time with the Romanian Ministry of Defense, my partner was also a military journalist in the late 1990s. Her report on our Everything PR News was but one neutral to positive report of several about the Russian leader. While Putin and Russia were only news for us, it's interesting to revisit today just how accurate and prophetic some of our analysis was back then.

In 2012 our engagement with Russia involved travel stories mostly. One human interest story set my eye on Sochi and the upcoming Olympics of 2014. A story about the Center for Dolphin Therapy in Russia, which is one of the many venues we've become known for publicizing over the years, got me focused on the environmental aspects of the Sochi Games. Some will remember that much of the news from back then was focused on Russia's development of the games infringing upon the wilderness.

Another facet that got me interested in Sochi was my own study of the 2010 Vancouver Olympics, and investigating for the serious concerns over a potential environmental catastrophe at that Olympics. Vancouver had its share of PR disasters including the First Nations native American lands controversy. More impactfully though, we reported on our Everything PR News an even more acute PR nightmare, the untimely death of Georgian luge athlete Nodar Kumaritashvili, who was tragically killed because of track experts claimed was too fast and deadly.

While this incident does not play a pivotal role in my work as a Kremlin "agent," the effort I personally made for Nodar's family, and for justice, it did set the stage. Ultimately, we uncovered many inconsistencies in the Olympic Committee's treatment of this accident, and our research led to companies from Germany and elsewhere that were riding the fringes of good business practices. Key people at the Olympics and NOC decision makers were not exactly above board in handing Nodar's death or in the way Vancouver went off. At those Olympics in Vancouver the International Olympic Committee (IOC), the International Luge Federation (FIL), and almost every official entity involved in the Nodar incident had failed athletes and the public miserably.

As far as I can remember, the outrage and reporting on this incident were the last time there was any consensus on truth from mainstream media in the West, at least as far as the Olympics are concerned. And while I did not fully realize it at the time, the disgraceful way Nodar and his family were treated, it had awakened the activist within me.

February 2014 was the year Phil Butler "sleeper agent" was

switched on by those pesky Russians. Or at least this is how some will eventually portray me. In all honesty, I have wondered many times why RTTV called to asked me to go on live television the same day Vladimir Putin opened the Sochi Olympics. However, in doing my research for the book you are reading, the reason became crystal clear. I am sure I first got on Russian media's radar with a story I wrote about Sochi 2014 for the Epoch Times entitled *"What If Sochi Will Be Greater Than Great? A Prelude of Hope to the XXII Winter Olympiad."*

The day before Margarita Simonyan's team contacted me for an interview, I had posted another article about those upcoming Sochi Olympics. The piece covered the diatribe that the Western mainstream media was launching against the Russians. Once again, our influence with Everything PR News parlayed the dissenting view. The power of this small media voice showed the negative PR campaigns, and cast Putin and Russia in a clear and more positive light. The story, *"Time, Richard Stengel, and Time for Better Russia Messaging"* involved TIME magazine's former editor Richard Stengel, and his wielding of the blunt tool of propaganda for President Barack Obama as Under Secretary of State for Public Diplomacy and Public Affairs. In short, I had exposed Stengel and TIME as being part of the greater anti-Russia media cabal. I distinctly remember quoting Vladimir Putin on western claims he was homophobic and that gay athletes at Sochi would be in danger:

"Just leave the children alone, please."
Russian President Vladimir Putin

The 2014 Sochi Olympics were a brilliant spectacle put on by the Russian people, and most saw though an unprecedented negative media campaign was leveled against the sporting event. After my RT interview, I joined the world in witnessing the nastiest and most scandalous propaganda assault ever undertaken. A shining moment for hundreds of wonderful athletes was transformed into a media circus – a circus with very powerful ringmasters in charge.

I watched from Germany on BBC, and Olympic spectacle that was at once thrilling and magnificent, and at the same time the saddest moment in my life as an athlete. The BBC and most other Western media reported on stray dogs, non-functional toilets, the plight of gays in Sochi bars, and left out or convoluted anything positive about the scene in Sochi.

For my team and me this was onerous, given we had colleagues on the ground in Sochi who were covering events. The spectacle that was a great Olympics left us feeling as if we witnessed a murder on closed circuit TV and the trial judge excluded our testimony. In the end, the "murderers" of the Sochi Olympics went free.

American President Barack Obama led the empire's unsportsmanlike conduct toward the Olympics in 2014. He was joined by the entire LGBT community of the western world. They even pulled lesbian tennis legend Billy Jean King out of mothballs just to become the poster girl of anti-Russian sports. In the end, the world's journalists missed no opportunity to cast a shadow over Russia's effort.

Reporters were instructed to dig for dirt and dig they did. Anytime a US athlete took a spill on the slopes, a news team was there to talk about bad snow conditions. If a Russian won a medal and an American did not, the whining and crying and bitching and moaning did not stop. From a sportsman's perspective watching Sochi was like watching athletics and the Olympic dream being flushed down a toilet. The horrendous coverage by American networks was only exceeded in nastiness by the BBC.

One moment that showed the British network's biased coverage came when Jenny Jones won Great Britain's first Olympic medal on snow in the snowboarding competition. In the booth for BBC were British snowboarder Aimee Fuller joined by Ed Leigh and Tim Warwood. The announcers were heard by viewers cheering when Jones's competitors fell. Fans of the sport complained to BBC about the lack of sportsmanship, which led to the article on the subject.

This was not an isolated event, I assure you. Oliver Brown of The Telegraph captured the distasteful essence of the BBC's unsportsmanlike partisanship:

> "In particular, the squeals from Fuller's

gormless sidekicks, Ed Leigh and Tim Warwood, both imploring Jones's Austrian rival Anna Gasser to fall over, were quite hog-whimperingly awful. It was the point at which patriotic zealousness tipped over into zealotry."

Russians whom I know were good sports, my young colleagues, photographers Pasha Kovalenko and Nina Zotina, took it upon themselves to go overboard photographing Olympic events for us. In all honesty, it was these two young Russians who opened my eyes to just how tragic the media war on Russia was. You see, we could not afford to pay much for photographers or reporters at the games, but these two young professionals were ever trusting and professional, and they ended up donating much of their time and effort to our cause of showing Sochi realistically. These two, and a scattering of other colleagues and associates of theirs, all proved the real spirit of Russians in a test which they never knew was a test.

Looking back, I wonder how any of us could have known that the Sochi Olympics smear campaign was just a diversion for the big show, for the Ukraine civil war to come. In this regard I shall never forget Pasha messaging me one day to ask, "Phil, do you think there will be war in Ukraine? I am afraid because I have family there." Like most people living in the west of Europe, I had no idea a new revolution was getting underway in Kiev.

It wasn't long before we all learned to be scared. US senators, the US ambassador and even senior US State Department personnel helped set Ukraine on fire. The February 2014 coup d'état began just as Vladimir Putin and Russia were focused on sport and the coming out party of Russia.

I wonder at the global view from Washington DC as I write this, and I shudder to think of the calculated recklessness of it all. That was a tipping point to make us question what US pretensions about freedom and democracy really mean.

Beneath the deafening noise of rocket fire across Donetsk and Luhansk, many of us found brothers and sisters fighting not just for peace, but for the essence of freedom itself. Make no mistake, the false narratives we are subjected to regarding Ukraine are signposts of freedom and democracy deconstructed and destroyed. It is in this fearsome reality the reader can find the real motivational component that serves "so-called" Kremlin Trolls. In the chapters to come the deep dark secrets of Vladimir Putin's harbingers will be unmasked. The hard lesson for most will be accepting a new reality.

Chapter II: The Low Blows in Sochi

"Russia never lost the Cold War... because it
never ended."
Vladimir Putin

The Sochi media debacle usurped my time so much that it took a few days for me to catch up with the events surrounding Euromaidan in Ukraine. "In shock" is the best way for me to describe my reaction to Ukrainians killing their own countrymen. The Kiev spectacle was surreal, highlighted by US officials like Senator John McCain looking on from hotel rooms like luxury sky boxes at a Super Bowl game. If the 2014 Winter Olympics displayed creepy poor sportsmanship, the carnage on Maidan Nezalezhnosti ("Independence Square") was societal destruction. The mix of graphic violence, the strange blend of celebrity with politics, and the western media bias were unbelievable. When I revisited the scene later to conduct research for this book, the moment still seems surreal.

Before the 2014 Ukraine revolution, I had sworn off political writing for good. I was determined to let my degree in political science collect dust because of the seeming hopelessness of world politics. The endless philosophizing that political scientists seem to thrive on seemed futile then, and it still does now. The political systems of the past two millennia represent for me humanity's most flawed endeavors, redeemed only by the fact that we have been unable to come up with any better solutions.

However, the Ukraine *coup d'état* represented a dire wound to the flesh of the "Rus". The sociopolitical damage we saw taking place had catastrophic implications. I recall having just written a travel piece about Ukraine, and I thought of colleagues from Ukraine and Russia whose families were caught up in the cruelty of the violent revolution there. To remain neutral in the wake of those terrible events, given my understanding of geopolitics, would have been cowardice.

At the moment of regime change in Ukraine, I had no media outlet or collaboration with which to share my opinions. At the time, my partner and I were in negotiations for selling our most influential media property Everything PR News. So, no matter what my research or opinions might be worth, there simply were all too few portals to write for. Nonetheless, on February 26, I decided to address this revolution via one of the most influential social media outlets of the time, Social Media Today[1]. In my report, I attempted to raise public awareness to both sides of the arguments. I recall now that President Obama called for "calm", while of course US agents in Ukraine financing the foreign fascist elements and directing the coup only made matters worse. At the time of this posting I had not considered the possibility that pro-Russia narrative might cause my business

---

[1] The Ukraine Revolt: Observations from the Social Side, by Phil Butler, February 26, 2015

any difficulty. Later, I would learn that Silicon Valley and the ecosystem the technocrats had created would shun any such prerogatives.

Throughout the spring of 2014, most of my own effort to report on the war in the Donbass and the overall geopolitical spectrum was via social media. My family and our travel news team were in Crete for the whole month of April and part of March, and the intensity of news out of Ukraine was felt less. Even after our crew returned to Germany, we felt a kind of helplessness over the awful killing in Ukraine. We were especially struck by the escalation of political tensions in the US, Britain and Europe towards Russia.

Added to this frustration was the fact that mainstream media I was writing for were not even looking for moderate news on Russia. Outlets like Huffington Post and Epoch Times were either mute or anti-Russia from the start. So, I continued along the contextual path via Everything PR News. In June, a piece entitled *"On Ukraine: A People Caught In a New 'Lebensraum'"* got a good deal of syndication by independent media like World News Daily.

The republishing of my Everything PR News story following the election of Petro Poroshenko showed me there was grassroots opposition to the western narrative. My story said, "old hatreds, fears, and divisions have been awakened", and that observation resonated. However, a quote from my Russian photographer friend from Sochi, Pasha Kovalenko, best characterized the injustice of Euromaidan:

"We are not part of Europe or America, yet we were taught that they are friends. This is why we always meet and greet these people, either here or on their land, with bread and smiles. Look how American culture has been adopted in our everyday life. We wear the jeans and sweatshirts, go to see the movies, and adore freedom like the Americans do. How can Russians now be cast as enemies?"

I cannot put enough stress on the fine character of this young Russian artist, and cadre of other unbelievable Russian youth who helped us tell about the real Sochi Olympics. Pasha is a good kid, a dedicated young talent with a beautiful family, who trusted an American, sight unseen. It is vital that the reader understands how true-blue most Russians we've come into contact with really are. While praising the Russian people is not what this book is all about, the motivations and reasoning behind pro-Russia activists from abroad do hinge on this. Pasha and his contemporary RIA photographer Nina Zotina exemplify all that is right with Vladimir Putin's country.

Looking back on the report, it was one of the best analytical pieces I had written since college. It was at this point the pro-Kiev media started labeling me as a "Putin apologist" and later an "MH17 truther" because of my research and analysis of the MH17 provocation and tragedy. When MH17 was shot down, all hell broke loose in mainstream media in the west. Russia and Vladimir Putin were immediately blamed, and a new kind of war began in earnest.

In the interim between Sochi and MH17, the ghastly imagery of the Odessa Massacre angered and captivated many of us. Not having access to the so-called "free press" to speak out about Ukrainian Nazis murdering unarmed protesters by burning them alive, I turned once again to contextualizing the event on our Everything PR News. It was at this point that I became acquainted with people who would become the most influential faces of the Ukraine/Crimea crisis via social media.

The Everything PR story about Odessa was a reach and, collaborating with many of these voices as a way to express my own distaste for the Kiev supported slaughter, it became clear a kind of "brotherhood" of moderators came in to being. By reflecting each other's research, views, and sometimes even ire, this budding community came to be in massive conflict with what was once called "traditional media."

Reporters like Graham Phillips, with his gripping videos, Marcel Sardo on Twitter, and the authors and volunteers from media outlets like Russia Insider, The Vineyard of The Saker, and Dr. Michel Chossudovskys' Global Research, all began to gravitate to the same spheres of conversation and information gathering. After a time, most of us who had been used to watching CNN or BBC started tuning to RT and shows like Peter Lavelle's *CrossTalk*, Abby Martin's *Breaking the Set*, and Anissa Naouai's *In the Now*.

As the diversity of views at western media outlets narrowed, those of us with dissenting views coalesced naturally toward the more open and transparent information channels. Yes, RT is a Russian state-funded broadcast company, but compared with Germany's ARD and other similar Western media, the Russian version of government TV was and is the voice of reason. A poignant anecdote here should suffice to show this.

Sometime in 2016 my colleague Holger Eekhof and I had a Skype call with RT news producer Maria Kvantrishvili about a news story Eekhof had uncovered. Maria, who was the producer the ever-popular RT show *In the Now* with my friend Anissa Naouai, was quizzing Eekhof and I about a Brussels parliament fiasco. Ever the smart and funny spirit, Maria is possessed of so many warm traits, one of the sweetest being a touch of what Americans would call "blondeness", even though she has stunning dark hair. In a Skype exchange regarding a possible RTTV story we were pitching, we related to Maria how Brussels had created its own "Fake News". The conversation revolved around the documentation EU parliamentarians were using to justify establishing an agency to counter alleged Russian anti-EU propaganda, which included only American and European sources for justification. After Eekhof and I suggested that the EU parliament was apparently operating just like CNN, Maria solemnly asked, "Don't they double check their facts?"

Both Eekhof and I immediately burst into uncontrollable

laughter in unison. Then, once we collected ourselves, there on the PC monitor we saw Maria's sweet and quizzical sideways stare. Her cheeks turned slightly rosy beneath her recent suntan. Her lips pursed in a familiar smirk, she could not help but bark at us like we were errant schoolboys, "What? - she urged." We gently explained to her that CNN often doesn't bother to check facts and that most western media now simply makes up facts. The moment was at once both ironic and perfect. After all the "fake news" we'd witnessed in the western media, one of RT's top producers exhibited in her innocence the admirable journalistic integrity of her media company.

German Chancellor Angela Merkel's "Truth Ministry", along with noted EU parliamentarian Elmar Brok (the man they call "Mr. Bertelsmann") were the focus of a later article by me on New Eastern Outlook[2]. As for RTTV, the network would later run a story about an EU Commission vote in Strasbourg. But what Eekhof and I remember most these days is the honest and girlishly innocent Kvantrishvili, who demonstrated RT's honesty and respect for truth.

As we look back now, we see clearly that most western media do not even "single check" their facts. The Daily Beast comes to mind, or the CNN executive caught admitting that CNN hammers on the anti-Russia narrative merely for the sake of ratings. Government TV, indeed. If Kvantrishvili is

---

[2]   *The "Godfather's" Address to the EU: An "Offer That Cannot Be Refused",* by Phil Butler, New Eastern Outlook, December 6, 2016

representative of that government owned media, give us more Russians.

Returning to the period after the Sochi Olympics had entered the history books, the #Odessa hashtag dominated Euromaidan, Euromaidan PR, and Euromaidan press all through the month of May 2014. I mention this here because it was the anti-Russian movement that took over social and traditional media first. This is a fact that no one has mentioned so far, to my knowledge. It is evidence for my ongoing contention that Vladimir Putin and Russia only reacted to pressure from Western influences. I will always believe Putin and his advisers were a bit surprised at the preemptive attack on two fronts. This is further revealed in that incensed pro-Russian and moderate engagement started later, in reaction to virulent anti-Russian provocation.

Looking back, it seems clear to me that much of the Euromaidan public relations and media effort was planned, which further illustrates my point. I also recall that almost magically the BBC and all the other western media were all but absent at this moment, except to label Russian sympathizers as aggressors, when they weren't busy blaming the pro-Russian victims for their own suffering.

When the British broadcasting giant did report on the massacre, its rhetoric only served to galvanize pro-Russia outrage and polarize the Ukraine unrest even further. One report from May 4 illustrates the one-sided blame-game the BBC helped propagate in the following months and years.

The trend of blaming the victims for letting themselves be injured and killed took hold then. BBC's David Stern reported from Odessa:

> *"The clashes underscored the passivity - and possible disloyalty - of Ukraine's police forces, who stood by and watched the mayhem unfold, and, if video footage is to be believed, provided cover for pro-Russian protesters shooting at, and killing, pro-Ukrainians."*

At this point, it seemed appropriate for most of us "Putin agents" to perceive our "opposition" as the journalists with clear vested interests in supporting Euromaidan. David L. Stern, the independent journalist reporting from Odessa, was later accused of being a CIA agent complicit in the shooting down of MH17. Audio files allegedly submitted by the ex-head of the Security Service of Ukraine (SBU) Valentyn Nalyvaichenko after his resignation were a huge point of contention at the time. The now notorious Eliot Higgins (aka Bellingcat) went to great lengths to try to debunk these claims, which in turn clarified the pro-Russian side of these arguments. Certainly, anything Higgins would later try to prove or disprove provided added impetus for many of us. The western media promoting Bellingcat "proofs" suggested to us that MH17 was probably a false flag operation or at least a huge lie. With no conclusive evidence available that proves who was responsible, all anyone has to go on is circumstantial and anecdotal evidence. This is true even to this day.

Returning to my role as one of Russia's top social media spooks (tongue in cheek), the "Odessa" story I wrote has been removed by the new owners of the Everything PR News outlet. The article, which I believe can still be found in internet archives, was significant because it was my first analysis of how western media from BBC to Euromaidan PR played their roles in anti-Russia propaganda. It was after this story, along with a massive social media stunt on my part, that I began to be sought out as a media analyst by the Russians and independent media. At this point Dutch national living in Germany Holger Eekhof, a friend, colleague and somewhat unsung pro-Russia hero played a major role behind the scenes. His role will become clearer in later chapters, but I distinctly recall our mutual disgust and ire over seeing those charred bodies in Odessa. For the next two months, we consumed every scrap of media and consulted one another almost daily on the degenerating chaos in Ukraine. From my American point of view, I found it hard to believe that what I saw was happening. Then the horror story turned nightmarish when Malaysia Airlines flight 17 (MH17) was shot down on July 17, 2014.

Starting July 18, 2014, I began using every social media tool at my disposal to try to find out who was responsible for a Boeing 777-200ER being blown from the sky over eastern Ukraine. The stream of information and data from July throughout the rest of 2014 was almost unimaginable, not to mention career and life changing. Ukraine was an uncontrollable disaster before 298 innocent passengers and crew were slain, but the world edged closer to Armageddon afterward.

I find it interesting now to scan my Facebook history and see my first reactions to the catastrophe. A Daily Mail report on President Barack Obama mentioning MH17 in a speech on transportation was a post only one other person "liked." The very early "activists" stirred up over the Ukraine Civil War that still runs today ranged from Russian expats to political scientists, students and social media regulars who were aghast at the sudden departure from relative harmony the west shared with Russia after the fall of the Soviet Union. It's fair to say that fear and then loathing of the disinformation war created a grassroots opposition to the anti-Russia line.

I remember that it was through Margo Beutel and others like her that many "Kremlin Trolls" became loosely connected. Then there were others like my own technology connections, who at first showed a moderate stance on Ukraine, but then later disappeared from my timeline altogether. Some expressed their doubts as to the validity of early US State Department claims, but then stopped voicing their opinions to avoid controversy. As for me, I began hammering Obama administration officials and media like Defense IQ for their accusative and unsubstantiated claims just hours after the aircraft crashed.

Owing to the reach of my personal and business social media influence, I expect my opinionated shares had some Putin-positive impact even early on. The second person to comment on an MH17 Facebook post of mine was not even a friend, but a man named Sarfaraz Ahmed from Islamabad. This Facebook person is interesting here because his "liking" of that particular post illustrates the vast importance of social media for both Moscow and Washington in this war of information. In short, internet connected social media reach an audience so powerful that we now see efforts by Germany and the EU aimed at censoring or controlling it[i].

Even before the Malaysian Airlines provocation, I had begun analysis of the underlying causes of renewed America-Russia conflict. A Quartz piece I shared on Facebook, and my argumentation with it, brought to the forefront the cliché "war for gas" machination. *"Putin's revenge—anti-fracking protests in Europe"* showed us a kind of template for future Obama administration led propaganda against Russia. This quote from the Steve LeVine Quartz[3] story reveals what I mean:

> *"In a London appearance on June 19, Anders Rasmussen, the secretary-general of NATO, accused Russia of secretly funding European non-governmental organizations (NGOs) that oppose hydraulic fracturing (or "fracking"), the method used to drill for shale gas, on environmental grounds. The objective,*

---

[3] *Putin's revenge—anti-fracking protests in Europe,* by Steve LeVine, Quartz, June 20, 2014.

according to Rasmussen: to frustrate European countries' efforts to wean themselves off Russian gas, which now comprises 30% of the European market."

My fellow Kremlin "agents" will cringe at the mere mention of Rasmussen's name, for NATO's former head accusing Russia of Soros-like NGO insurgency is truly the "pot calling the kettle black." This kind of rhetorical redirect would become the nauseatingly familiar strategy of western world leaders. But before I reveal the deeper network of pro-Russian activists and "operatives," a close friend and colleague of mine needs to be revealed.

From the early stages of my own geopolitical studies, my friend Holger Eekhof has played a significant role in my own research and in voicing dissent across commentary channels. A Dutch national, Eekhof has lived in Germany most of his life and was once a CDU politician. Today he offers a keen insight, especially from the German perspective, on geopolitics and European law. I mention Eekhof for two reasons. First and foremost, he has been analyzing this anti-Russia situation since before the 2008 South Ossetia War, which makes him one of the longest living Kremlin Trolls (by definition). More importantly for this book though, it was Eekhof who prompted me back in June 2014, to begin looking hard at the "natural gas" aspect of the whole Ukraine affair. Eekhof's initial media studies focused on the German ZEIT and other quasi-intellectual German media, which would later prove invaluable in compiling information on the key players behind this crisis. I distinctly remember Eekhof and I discussing Ukraine, and Crimea in particular, about natural gas and its influence on world energy markets. It was Eekhof who reminded me of the immense importance of transit and supply on this subject, in particular, the need for storage and "regasification" facilities.

Interestingly, an Everything PR News story in which I discussed this "energy" facet has since disappeared from the Everything PR News website. I'll get into why I think it vanished later, but luckily the story has been archived elsewhere on the web. In "Ukraine, Arab Spring, Cold War II and Price Wars Hardly Disguised" the nexus of what we've come to call the "New Democratic Order" is featured prominently. This quote from my conclusions hints at what I'll later reveal as the true enemy of the Kremlin:

> *"I imagine a world of business actions, running wholesale and almost chaotically the fate of billions of human beings. This is the "obtuse" garden where billionaires get too busy and maybe too dumb to really act smartly. The alternative view leaves us with evil bastards who could care less about the environment, people, or even their own legacy. The coming race to capitalize on all the world's shale natural gas will be something greater than even the California gold rush."*

Now it seems appropriate to introduce a rather "naked" Kremlin troll, an operative truly in the trenches of this asymmetric media war. Eekhof inhabits the comment sections of some of the world's most influential media, media such as ZEIT. The man who now blogs at Sputnik, started off his pro-Russia endeavors in the most organic of ways – his life partner being from Tbilisi, and their network of friends including many Russians in Germany. As for our relationship, Eekhof and I share many common interests, not the least of which being geography, history, and a special kind of anti-Russophobia angst. In the coming chapters, you'll find this top Kremlin Troll mentioned sporadically along with others but remember this "regasification" story, along with Vice President Joe Biden's son signing on with Burisma Holding[4], is central to understanding the truth of Ukraine and the regime changes we've witnessed since the Arab Spring began.

One common denominator you will find in the profiles of Kremlin Trolls you will discover here, is the fervent idealism heated to a boiling point be real and perceived injustices. In Holger Eekhof's case, his life partner being from the Bagrationi family of the Republic of Georgia added a kind of reality most people cannot see. So, this influence has an organically positive effect on the way Eekhof and this whole circle of friends viewed the aforementioned war in South Ossetia. The reader should understand that the real people

---

4   *Joe Biden, His Son and the Case Against a Ukrainian Oligarch"* - Hunter Biden sits on the board of one of Ukraine's largest natural gas companies. The New York Times

of these former Soviet republics have their fond memories too. Georgia being one of the most privileged republics, led to much closer ties between modern Georgia and Russia than Westerners are led to believe. His natural inclinations and expertise within the realm of CDU and European political study were fed by grassroots and credible local opinion and ideas. My point here is that Georgia's leadership often reflects one view, while the people in the streets genuinely reflect another. Eekhof's view is extremely important for this very reason – he mirrors the real-world view tempered by his knowledge of all the legalities of policy building.

For this key Kremlin Troll analyst, the game started as an intellectual pastime as far back as 2002, and after the Euromaidan changed from being a secondary hobby to a full-time job. Eekhof read and commented on online German news and periodicals out of his interest in litigation and policy from his CDU days. Later, he tells me, German media like ZEIT and many others simply became propaganda instruments. What I found far more interesting though something Eekhof said about the local and national level CDU hierarchy: recently how deep-seated Russophobia existed in the Trier "club," as well as higher up at every level of the organization. Eekhof said the leadership at the local offices even accused his Russian girlfriend at the time of being a "Russian spy." This story is not a unique one, I assure you.

Having lived in this region a decade now, the shadows of the distant past still loom large over the land and the German psyche. Even today Eekhof cannot believe the utter stupidity and narrow-mindedness his CDU colleagues showed toward Russians, in fact, he told me many times this narrow view was the reason he left the party for good. On reflection, I see more clearly commonality among almost all foreign pro-Russia activists in disenchantment. This is not about so-called Kremlin Trolls being disenfranchised, but about idealism and the disappointment that comes from encountering the warped politics. As Eekhof said once:

> "I could not believe how stupid and short sighted they were, Phil. And all of them."

He was referring to CDU and other party officials even up to the highest level. From what he describes, the essence of the "party" is really like a country club, or perhaps those Moose Lodges from my American experience. Now that I think about Eekhof's recounting of events in the Trier CDU club, I think the "Loyal Order of Water Buffaloes" from the cartoon The Flintstones, where Fred Flintstone and Barney Rubble were members of the lodge, may be more accurate. Germany does have its share of villages that could as easily be called Bedrock, the socialism here being orchestrated over the top of some really archaic thinking masked as democracy. While the reader is surely more interested in how other actors and I were "recruited" for their alleged roles in the coming Dezinformatsiya, German politics and Eekhof come up frequently later in the book.

Up until the time of the MH17 tragedy, my role in moderating anti-Russia sentiment was almost entirely confined to social media. Then, on July 17, 2014, the proverbial shit hit the fan. Stunned like everyone else, I immediately turned to traditional media, only to get the immediate sense that a media control game was in place. Then, in rapid succession, RTTV called to ask my opinion on the PR at work against Russia, and social media lines went buzzing like crazy.

Supposedly recorded communications, real and fake video, and every manner of contrivance was pitted against the blatantly obvious about the downed Malaysian airliner. A blame game of never before seen magnitude ensued to the west, with political celebrities like the US Secretary of State John Kerry, Hillary Clinton on the Charley Rose Show, and soon to be famous (or infamous) journos like Eliot Higgins (aka *Bellingcat) and Daily Beast's Michael Weiss.*

On the other end of the "arguments" over who shot this airliner down, some names would become synonymous with the euphemism "Kremlin Troll." From Global Research's Professor Michel Chossudovsky's initial report the flight path of MH17 had been changed, to what soon became a small legion of pro-Russian supporters, the reason seemed to demand a questioning and moderating counterbalance to the American propaganda.

An almost immediate analysis by urban legend Andrei Raevsky, better known as "The Saker" because of his intensely critical and well-documented works at The Vineyard of The Saker website, led the foray into independent analysis of the event. The absence of real evidence by the US administration, the disjointed and strange accusations of the Poroshenko government, and parroting across the media spectrum in America and Europe provoked a natural counter-response. For my part, the RT interview led to some Russian media amplifying my later writings, and I did a short stint writing op-ed material for the RT website. *"Death & lies: The only truth of flight MH17"* in late August was a reflection of the overall frustration many people felt for the total lack of proof presented on the disaster.

As an interesting footnote here, RT's Op-Edge editor, Natalia Makarova had offered me normal compensation for my editorials according to industry standards, but I turned down them down for what were for me obvious reasons. It might interest the reader to know that this condemned Putin Troll has never received compensation from RT, Russia One, NTV, Russia 24, RIA Novosti, or Pravda for dozens of editorials or TV appearances. This is not to suggest some journalists accused of being Kremlin agents do not get paid for their work, I simply mention it here because so many who are unpaid have been so accused.

Chapter III: A Solitary Falcon

*"Sometimes it is necessary to be lonely
in order to prove that you are right."*
Vladimir Putin

I have already related how me and some other players became involved in what some people call the *New McCarthyism*. From here on I will also discuss how I came to be acquainted with most all of the most notorious pro-Russia figures, the people otherwise known as *Kremlin fanboys and fangirls*. But as famous and familiar as the names and faces of most of the analysts, journalists, and social media people taking Russia's part are, there's one iconic dissenter who's more prescient than all the rest. At this point, it seems appropriate to introduce one of the most famous Kremlin Trolls, the self-proclaimed "Putin Fanboy" known as The Saker. With his permission, I include the first of several confessed Kremlin Troll autobiographies. What you are about to read comes directly from the source, The Vineyard of The Saker website at http://thesaker.is.

How I became a Kremlin troll by The Saker

By birth, experience, and training, I truly had everything needed to hate Putin. I was born in a family of "White Russians" whose anti-Communism was total and visceral.

My childhood was filled with (mostly true) stories about atrocities and massacres committed by the Bolsheviks during the revolution and subsequent civil war. Since my father had left me, I had an exiled Russian Orthodox Archbishop as a spiritual father, and through him, I learned of all the genocidal persecutions the Bolsheviks unleashed against the Orthodox Church.

At the age of 16, I had already read the three volumes of the "Gulag Archipelago" and carefully studied the history of WWII. By 18 I was involved in numerous anti-Soviet activities such as distributing anti-Soviet propaganda in the mailboxes of Soviet diplomats or organizing the illegal importation of banned books into the Soviet Union through the Soviet merchant marine and fishing fleet (mostly at their station in the Canary Islands). I was also working with an undercover group of Orthodox Christians sending help, mainly in the form of money, to the families of jailed dissidents. And since I was fluent in Russian, my military career took me from a basic training in electronic warfare, to a special unit of linguists for the General Staff of the Swiss military, to becoming a military analyst for the strategic intelligence service of Switzerland.

The Soviet authorities had long listed me, and my entire family, as dangerous anti-Soviet activists and I, therefore, could not travel to Russia until the fall of Communism in 1991 when I immediately caught the first available flight and got to Moscow while the barricades built against the GKChP coup were still standing. Truly, by this fateful month of August 1991, I was a perfect anti-Soviet activist and an anti-

Communist hardliner. I even took a photo of myself standing next to the collapsed statue of Felix Derzhinsky (the founder of the ChK - the first Soviet Secret police) with my boot pressed on his iron throat. That day I felt that my victory was total. It was also short-lived.

Instead of bringing the long-suffering Russian people freedom, peace, and prosperity, the end of Communism in Russia only brought chaos, poverty, violence, and abject exploitation by the worst class of scum the defunct Soviet system had produced. I was horrified. Unlike so many other anti-Soviet activists who were also Russophobes, I never conflated my people and the regime which oppressed them. So, while I rejoiced at the end of one horror, I was also appalled to see that another one had taken its place. Even worse, it was undeniable that the West played an active role in every and all forms of anti-Russian activities, from the total protection of Russian mobsters, on to the support of the Wahabi insurgents in Chechnya, and ending with the financing of a propaganda machine which tried to turn the Russian people into mindless consumers to the presence of western "advisors" (yeah, right!) in all the key ministries. The oligarchs were plundering Russia and causing immeasurable suffering, and the entire West, the so-called "free world" not only did nothing to help but helped all the enemies of Russia with every resource it had. Soon the NATO forces attacked Serbia, a historical ally of Russia, in total violation of the most sacred principles of international law. East Germany was not only reunified but instantly incorporated into West Germany and NATO pushed as far East as possible. I could not pretend that all this could be explained by some fear of the Soviet military or by a reaction to the Communist theory of world revolution. In truth, it became clear to me that the western elites did not hate the Soviet system or ideology, but that they hated Russian people themselves and the culture and civilization which they had created.

By the time the war against the Serbian nation in Croatia, Bosnia and Kosovo broke out, I was in a unique situation: all day long I could read classified UNPROFOR and military reports about what was taking place in that region and, after work, I could read the counter-factual anti-Serbian propaganda the western corporate Ziomedia was spewing out every day. I was horrified to see that literally everything the media was saying was a total lie. Then came the false flags, first in Sarajevo, but later also in Kosovo. My illusions about "Free World" and the "West" were crumbling. Fast.

Fate brought me to Russia in 1993 when I saw the carnage of meted out by the "democratic" Eltsin regime against thousands of Russians in Moscow (many more than what the official press reported). I also saw the Red Flags and Stalin portraits around the parliament building. My disgust by then was total. And when the Eltsin regime decided to bring Dudaev's Chechnia to heel triggering yet another needless bloodbath, that disgust turned into despair. Then came the stolen elections of 1996 and the murder of General Lebed. At that point, I remember thinking "Russia is dead."

So, when the entourage of Eltsin suddenly appointed an unknown nobody to acting President of Russia, I was rather dubious, to put it mildly. The new guy was not a drunk or an arrogant oligarch, but he looked rather unimpressive. He was also ex-KGB which was interesting: on one hand, the KGB had been my lifelong enemy but on the other hand, I knew that the part of the KGB which dealt with foreign intelligence was staffed by the brightest of the brightest and that they had nothing to do with political repression, Gulags and all the rest of the ugly stuff another Directorate of the KGB (the 5th) was tasked with (that department had been abolished in 1989). Putin came from the First Main Directorate of the KGB, the "PGU KGB." Still, my sympathies were more with the (far less political) military intelligence service (GRU) than the very political PGU which, I was quite sure by then, had a thick dossier on my family and me.

Then, two crucial things happened in parallel: both the "Free world" and Putin showed their true faces: the "Free world" as an AngloZionist Empire hell-bent on aggression and oppression, and Vladimir Putin as a real patriot of Russia. In fact, Putin slowly began looking like a hero to me: very gradually, in small incremental steps first, Putin began to turn Russia around, especially in two crucial matters: he was trying to "re-sovereignize" the country (making it truly sovereign and independent again), and he dared the unthinkable: he openly told the Empire that it was not only wrong, it was illegitimate (just read the transcript of Putin's amazing 2007 "Munich Speech").

Putin inspired me to make a dramatic choice: will I stick to my lifelong prejudices or will I let reality prove my lifelong prejudices wrong. The first option was far more comfortable to me, and all my friends would approve. The second one was far trickier, and it would cost me the friendship of many people. But what was the better option <u>for Russia</u>? Could it be that it was the right thing for a "White Russian" to join forces with the ex-KGB officer?

I found the answer here in a photo of Alexander Solzhenitsyn and Vladimir Putin:

If that old-generation anti-Communist hardliner who, unlike me, had spent time in the Gulag, could take Putin's hand, then so could I!

In fact, the answer was obvious all along: while the "White" and the "Red" principles and ideologies were incompatible and mutually exclusive, there is also no doubt that nowadays true patriots of Russia can be found both in the former "Red" and "White" camps. To put it differently, I don't think that "Whites" and "Reds" will ever agree on the past, but we can, and must, agree on the future. Besides, the Empire does not care whether we are "Red" or "White" - the Empire wants us all either enslaved or dead.

Putin, in the meantime, is still the only world leader with enough guts to openly tell the Empire how ugly, stupid and irresponsible it is (read his 2015 UN Speech). And when I listen to him I see that he is neither "White" nor "Red." He is simply Russian.

So, this is how I became a Kremlin troll and a Putin fanboy.

The Saker

In relating to his readers his emotional and professional essence, the most respected pro-Russian blogger of all refers to himself and by affiliation many other such idealists as "submarines in the desert." In a letter of gratitude to his throng of fans, he relates how his wife supported his "paying the price for his integrity," after standing up for his ideals. The Saker wrote:

> "In those dark days, my wonderful wife was always trying to tell me that it was not my fault, that I had never done anything wrong, that I was paying the price for being a person of integrity and that I had proven many times over how good I was in my field. I always used to bitterly reply to her that I was like a "submarine in a desert": maybe very good at "something somewhere," but useless in my current environment (I always used to visualize an Akula-class SSN stranded smack in the middle of the Sahara Desert."

Chapter IV: Against Dezinformatsiya

"Maybe they have nothing else to do in America
but to talk about me."
Vladimir Putin

Between the Sochi Olympics and the Odessa Massacre, much dissent began to pile up against the western narrative of the growing crisis in Ukraine too. When those poor people were barbecued alive by the angry mob at the Trade Unions House in Odessa, scattered pieces of those events began converging into a tangible truth. The puzzle began to materialize exactly in reverse of the US State Department and the Obama administration version. The imagery of US Senator John McCain, or the now infamous Under Secretary of State Victoria (Fuck the EU) Nuland, were galvanized directly into the minds of many. This was especially true for all who had seen the Bandera loyalists and neo-Nazis parading around Ukraine. McCain, Nuland, US Ambassador Geoffrey Pyatt, even the famous boxer Wladimir Klitschko were branded forever with the mark of the Wolfsangel[5], whether they liked being exposed as Nazi sympathizers or

---

[5]   The *Wolfsangel* was one of the first symbols of the Nazi Party, and was used by various Nazi German storm divisions such as the Waffen-SS Division Das Reich and the Waffen-SS Division Landstorm Nederland. *Himmler's SS: Loyal to the Death's Head (2009) Lumsden, Robin*

not. Propaganda and rampant Russophobia were being cultivated by the western media and distributed worldwide by this time.

Then the ultimate provocation was perpetrated – flight MH17 was shot down, allegedly by "Putin's missile", according to Kiev. Even before the wreckage had stopped smoldering, Washington's media machine went into action recreating the *Red Scare* all over again[6]. But in the Donbass in eastern Ukraine, a handful of brave souls presented us with more tangible evidence that contradicted most of the western mainstream media rhetoric. Media mavericks like Graham Phillips were on site for RT (Russia Today), and independent networks with war correspondent footage of the devastation happening daily and not just the day the Malaysian airliner crashed. The zeal and courage of a few activists bolstered many more to assume their roles as moderators and peacekeepers. This all occurred at a time when World War III almost seemed imminent. In retrospect, what a couple of dozen people managed to set in motion stunned the traditional media world.

Evidence to counter the western media onslaught was supplied by analysts like The Saker, RT contributors like Mark Sleboda, a handful of journalists like Graham Phillips and normal citizens like my colleagues Holger Eekhof and Paul Payer, and notable independent media like Consortium

---

[6] *The New Red Scare,* by Andrew Cockburn, Harpers, December, 2016

News, Global Research, Zero Hedge, and even at Katrina vanden Heuvel's *The Nation*. That information combined with the spurious media events coming out of Britain and America motivated me to become proactive and political too. The airline tragedy was the deep line in the sand in between the globalists and nationalists. Syria and later conflagrations notwithstanding, many began to see Russia under attack by western powers at this time. It was at this moment that I began investigating and relating what information I could glean, along with some thought provoking theories via our Everything PR News and some other independent media.

Then on July 21st RT's producers called me to do another interview on the MH17 airline catastrophe. During the interview, I was asked about the very early accusations against the separatists in Ukraine, and against Russia proper. I was also quizzed on what media's role should have been in reporting these events. Things like verified sources and double-checking facts came up, as they should have. As we see now "Fake News" ended up in a fever pitch after the Donald Trump won the US presidential election, but it's interesting to note that RT, the network accused most of being a "propaganda bullhorn", is the network that sought a modicum of journalistic appropriateness during this key crisis. In the interview, I condemned western leaders and media for replacing ironclad facts with "flimsy speculation". This criticism later proved prophetic when President Trump counterattacked what he termed "quasi-journalists" for reporting "Fake News". So, the reader gets a better picture of my "conversion" to the pro-Russia side of things, and my own litmus test for Russian media's legitimacy.

When I arrived at the Trier, Germany TV studio for this first interview I asked the technicians wiring me up, whether the interview was being recorded or not. "No, this is live", I remember him answering. This moment in my journey brings me to an interesting point I've expressed many times since. At such a significant moment for Russia why would the alleged propaganda ministry of the autocrat Vladimir Putin trust a good ol' boy from America to go live before its English-speaking audience? Each time I reflect on the interview I wonder what alternative reality I might have been part of. What if I decided to start bashing Sochi for some unseen environmental catastrophe? What if some western oligarch had paid me off to trash Mr. Putin's party? Innocence, honesty, straightforwardness by the RT people convinced me early on, that the narrative from the opposition was the message in the red.

Moving forward, it was after the MH17 provocation things began to change very quickly, both in my personal and business world and the world of geopolitics. As my writings and social media presence uncovered or mirrored the moderate view on Russia more and more, relationships and even business opportunities began drying up for our PR company.

At first, I thought lost opportunities were a function of my own diverted focus from PR or from my technical columns onto more politically motivated topics. Then a preponderance of negative feedback from my social and business network, and especially my media colleagues in the west, it convinced me of the obvious. Editors began to turn down news and editorial in any way supportive of Russia.

It was at this juncture RT's Op-Edge editors asked me to contribute a piece about the tragedy. *"Death & lies: The only truth of flight MH17"* had some stunning elements, and was eventually republished by many independent media outlets. The detail in this report that had the most impact was the stunning revelation former US Secretary of State Hillary Clinton was playing the financial markets on Rubles the instant MH17 disintegrated over Ukraine. Her interview with Charley Rose just hours after the crash got lost in the media frenzy that followed.

Whether I was "recruited" as a Kremlin agent by RT or not will probably always be a contentious point. For me, however, my association with the Russian TV and media network is a point of great pride for several reasons. First and foremost, when RT editors offered to pay me like any other journalist, I turned down any compensation so that my credibility and objectivity might stay intact. I saved the correspondence on this so that any such accusation could easily be addressed. Secondly, my role with RT has always hinged on pristine professional relations with everyone at the network. While I have never made any secret of my admiration or even friendship toward Margarita Simonyan and others there, I also refrained from such things as name dropping or even undue direct correspondence. As far as most RT employees or editors know, I'm just an analyst on their lists of sources to contact. This is the way I want it, in order that my efforts are as genuine and honest as possible.

Whatever readers choose to believe, subsequent events reveal the clear bias against anyone taking the moderate line on Russia. This bias reached a feverish pitch very early on in this new media war. As an example, a story on the Epoch Times I managed to get my colleagues there to publish, pretty much spelled the end of my blogging career at the popular site. In a cool bit of irony, it was me who was instrumental in helping the Senior Editor Jan Jekielek to launch Epoch Times' blogging community. So, when the leadership of the newspaper created and supported by Falun Gong[7] decided to do away with dozens of blogs overnight, you can imagine my chagrin. Conversations I had with both Jan Jekielek and his wife, Digital Chief Editor Cindy Drukier Jekielek never served to satisfy me as to the real reasons for all those blogs being shut down without prior notice. I must stress here, I still consider both people my friends, for they've time and again exhibited uncommon professionalism and kindness. This is another reason I am convinced something out of the ordinary took place behind closed doors. To this

---

[7]   Noakes, Stephen (June 2010). "Falun Gong, Ten Years On". *Pacific Affairs.* Pacific Affairs, a division of the University of British Columbia. 83 (2): 349–57.

day Epoch Times editorial and news stories are few and far between where Russia and Putin are concerned, and what there is inside the pages is basically parroting the mainstream. Given the nature of Epoch Times and the seeming independent voice it once was, I find this to be as telling as any Washington Post or Daily Beast anti-Putin tirade.

As far as I know, *"Malaysia Airlines Flight MH17 Investigation: Trail of Guarded Secrets"* is the most Russia neutral or positive article on any of the print or digital pages of Epoch Times since 2014. In the story, I cite a communication I had with the OSCE's spokesperson at the time, Cathie Burton that included her response to my frustration at the difficulty obtaining clear information from sources on either side of the MH17 situation:

> *"I understand your frustration: this is a difficult time to find the facts, and I have personally never seen so much misinformation spread, either mischievously or innocently."*

Epoch Times curiosities notwithstanding, other media really shied away from the heated controversy (or business) of even a moderate view on Russia. A post at Japan Today, followed by an email from my kind editor friend there, revealed the "unpopularity" of Russia sympathy. "Flight MH17: Will the world ever know the truth?" put an end to my political scribbling to the Japan Today audience. Other media batten down their hatches, so to speak, and a lot of visibility vanished for me and other authors. The point is, the reader here can more clearly see how Putin fans became the most notable - or notorious - media combatants for Russia. Ostracized for speaking any dissenting view on an array of crises and news, almost every so-called Kremlin Troll I know has experienced a similar situation. This is where the media battle lines were drawn. Late in 2014 those who initially questioned US State Department policy and propaganda lines became determined to fight the false narrative. It was during this time that "truth seekers" encountered the mass of vested media interests and the political and bureaucratic behemoth stacked up behind them. What we would later identify as a concrete mainstream media monstrosity encompassed all languages, continents, media and social strata.

At that time, my own understanding of the media war against Russia was quite naïve and innocent, just to be honest. While I understood how politically incorrect my views seemed to media I had previously worked for, the scope of literal control of western media still evaded me. The people and agencies pulling strings, their ultimate organizational structure, and their goals, these were obscured mostly by the unimaginable scope of the thing.

Before 2015 not many people could conceive of such media control. Orwell's book *1984* was still considered fiction by most people. The Edward Snowden revelations about the NSA had not yet been fully absorbed by the public either, so imagining a "deep state" propaganda machine extending across the world was simply not something even seasoned journalists or analysts focused on.

Then the independent media caught wind of NGOs and characters like billionaire George Soros, and learned that a broad network of subversive agencies had deeply embedded their claws into western society. In North America, across Europe, and especially in the former Soviet states, Soros and others had created a real subculture of anti-traditionalist, post-modernist liberalism. The "movement," if I may call it that, is also virulently anti-Russian.

While this aspect of my involvement is better suited to another book, the organizational aspect of this "network" is indicative of the long-range strategies leveled primarily at Russia. The Euromaidan and this whole anti-Russia circus we are witnessing were planned far in advance.

To put this "network" in better focus, it's important to understand the role of George Soros in Eastern Europe, and especially in Ukraine. The DCLeaks revelations that came out after Soros' NGO Open Society Foundations was hacked revealed what can only be described as a diabolical strategy for media and regime control. I recall an article on Zero Hedge[8] citing DCLeaks in 2016:

---

8   *George Soros Hacked, over 2,500 Internal Docs Released Online*, by Tyler Durden, Zero Hedge, August 16, 2016

"George Soros is a Hungarian-American business magnate, investor, philanthropist, political activist, and author who is of Hungarian-Jewish ancestry and holds dual citizenship. He drives more than 50 global and regional programs and foundations. Soros is named an architect and a sponsor of almost every revolution and coup around the world for the last 25 years."

Euromaidan Press, which very early on labeled anyone with an opposing view either Kremlin apologists or Putin trolls, is supported by George Soros' Renaissance Foundation. These media "arms" of the Soros machine take great pride in having been sourced by BBC, Reuters, The New York Times, and most Western mainstream media. Their constant harping about "troll armies" and Putin's so-called propaganda machine started the instant the Ukraine civil war began. The hysteria continues even as I write this chapter, and even more vociferously. One article entitled *"Kremlin trolls exposed: Russia's information war against Ukraine"* uses the same kind of "quasi-proof" CNN and other media are currently being bashed over. The cited article claims there are thousands of paid Kremlin trolls that have been identified by Ukrainian journalist Roman Kulchinskiy (recently mentioned by the Ukrainian version of Radio Free Europe/Radio Liberty). Furthermore, social activist Liudmyla Savchuk supposedly infiltrated this troll army to discover their social media dominance. The article quotes Savchuk:

"They're everywhere — Facebook, Vkontakte, LiveJournal, Odnoklassniki. They make their own fake news sites. They create their own news agencies. They pretend to be Ukrainian journalists. They write as if they're Ukrainian journalists. As if they're from Kyiv or Kharkiv, but they're really in Russia. They simply take a news piece, rewrite it how they need it, distort the information and send it out into the world."

A more recent case of Kremlin Troll hysteria can be found in an article by a girl named Morgan Chalfont, a recent Boston College grad who writes a cybersecurity column at Jimmy Finkelstein's political newspaper The Hill[9]. As an observation note here, Finkelstein is an immensely influential individual who some say is a "real nasty piece of work"[10]. Returning for the moment to the young reporter's August 2017 story, Chalfont cites quasi-experts about a supposed Kremlin smear campaign against US President Donald Trump's National Security Adviser H.R. McMaster. The straight out of college girl uses the dubious Atlantic Council Digital Forensic Research Lab and FireEye iSIGHT Intelligence. The reason I use the term "dubious" is because the Atlantic Council think tank makes no bones about its globalist stance, and because

---

[9] *James A. Finkelstein*, Bloomberg executive profile

[10] *Last Shoe Drops: The Hollywood Reporter's Jimmy Finkelstein Finally Removed — Is Sale Next?*, Nikki Finke, Deadline Hollywood, January 2015

of the twenty-five or more foreign countries that fund it. Russia is not one of those countries, just so my point is well made. As for FireEye, the Milpitas, California startup founded by new Pakistani billionaire Ashar Aziz was funded by Sequoia Capital, the investors largely responsible for Apple, Google, PayPal, YouTube, and Yahoo! Venture capital. The company is now run by former US Air Force officer Kevin Mandia, who has Silicon Valley venture ties to Kleiner Perkins Caufield & Byers, which is headed by the technocrats that boosted Google and Amazon to the forefront of the digital world. The reason I make these connections is to show the vested "interests" aspect from the technocrats' side of the whole Russia story. The Atlantic Council concocting narrative to suit geo-strategy is no new methodology, and companies selling stocks on Wall Street are certainly not above misleading the public. FireEye has been called out on more than one occasion as well[11]. As a "for instance", the independent media led by Zero Hedge utterly destroyed a Bloomberg story where FireEye accused Russia of "weaponizing" social media. The long and short of the anti-Russia narrative from Washington think tanks and intelligence community technocrats is, most of the evidence and all the dogma is invented. Let's look at the notion of "weaponized social media" from a first adopters point of

---

[11] *Bloomberg Reports Fake News: Story Claims FireEye Said Russia 'Weaponized Social Media' During Elections,* by The_Real_Fly, Zero Hedge, December 1, 2016

view.

I hope the reader will forgive me a brief digression into sarcasm here, but as the alleged top Kremlin troll on Earth, it seems to me I should know more about these "thousands" by now. In all seriousness, why don't each of my "Putin tweets" receive at least 100 retweets? Instead of using my own money for boosting Facebook posts featuring my articles, how is it my master's paid minions are not sharing on their own? The answer will become blazingly, alarmingly, and gloriously evident by the end of this book. According to Soros' paid minions, Vladimir Putin is spending upwards of $400,000 dollars a month at the legendary St. Petersburg troll factory alone! For those up us wired into the social media circuit board in this media war, the suggestion is preposterous for a multiplicity of reasons.

The reality of the St. Petersburg IT operation is a far more mundane like-share operation undertaken for good old capitalistic reasons. I have it on good advice that some innovative 'entrepreneur' in Russia does, in fact, get paid for social media "juice," but these are likes and shares for businesses, technology startups, and social media marketers, etc.

Once again, this is fodder for yet another book, but my point is made here. I was an early adopter when social media was very young. The marketing strategies of Facebook and Twitter and 100 others were in a small way, influenced by me and my contemporaries. Trust me, if there were 2,000

Kremlin trolls out there on Putin's payroll, I'd be one of the first beneficiaries of their influence. This Roman Kulchinskiy who was sourced by the CIA backed Radio Free Europe/Radio Liberty mimicked another well-known internet agent for the West, a man named Andrew Weisburd, who I shall discuss later. For Kulchinskiy's part, he and his colleagues supposedly used a social indexing tool[12] to "correlate" Kremlin toll associations. What is amazing for me is the fact none of the most prominent *Kremlin Troll* confessors in this book seems to be in this correlative matrix. As for this St. Petersburg troll army, I shall delve into the contrivance of this as a strategy later in the book. At this point it's just important to understand that there are strategies being played out before us.

---

12   *The Troll Network*, Texty.org, October 4, 2016

Chapter V: The Reagent - Russia Insider

"The attempts to distort the truth and to hide the facts behind blanket accusations have been undertaken at all stages of the Ukrainian crisis."
Sergei Lavrov

After the MH17 catastrophe, social media and so-called "non-traditional" media lit up in amplification of the new and fast growing west-east crisis. Publishers, editors, and ultimately readers were increasingly polarized in their views on the situation about US-Russia relations. As I've suggested, it would become abundantly clear pro-Russian voices would eventually be in a defensive battle against a massively funded and seemingly indomitable western mainstream foe. The "Putin Fanboys" or apologists, as we were so often called, would be forced into an increasingly bombastic and inflammatory media cataclysm.

Owing to the growing negative attitude toward Russia, any positive message sent across western mainstream media was at first discouraged, and then eventually disallowed altogether. For freelancers and independent journalists like myself, a virtual ban on positive Russia stories was in effect. Once I began writing Op-Ed for RT, the situation only grew worse. In November 2014, my story "25 Years after the Berlin Wall: Who really won the Cold War" struck a nerve for addressing the reality of Eastern Europe after the fall of the Soviet Union. The next day Euromaidan Press attacked me and the RT network for my comparisons in between slain US President John F. Kennedy and Russia President Vladimir Putin. An interview I gave as a PR expert was taken completely out of context in what would become the trend for all pro-Kiev stories. At that moment, I could not know that the broadcast would be my last appearance as Editor in Chief of Everything PR News.

On the PR and digital marketing side of things, we would end up losing half our clients over my prominent social media presence showing Russia's side of MH17 and the Donbass situation. On more than one occasion I was told; "Phil, the higher ups do not like the fact you are so pro-Russian." Before long, this political variable would force us to sell Everything PR News. Late 2014 and early 2015 was a low point for our small business, and for me as publisher and independent writer.

The events that followed forged me and others into media guerrillas. The term "Kremlin Troll" would come to represent a badge of honor for anyone with a clear vision of the battlefield. It was not the Russians who destroyed détente and prevented cooperation and commerce through compromise, it was the American hegemony that waged a media war seeking domination.

For me another crucial point came when the founder of the rapidly growing independent website Russia Insider asked me to become the publisher of the dissenting media outlet. American businessman Charles Bausman's editors had previously contacted me to contribute some of my articles to their website to counter NATO propaganda rhetoric. After meeting with Bausman personally, I agreed to join what was the most amazing volunteer organization I'd ever been involved with, an organization that until now has been misunderstood.

It was Bausman, whose father was the AP bureau chief in Moscow during the height of the Cold War, who at that time represented the tip of the sword of pro-Russia media. While Russia Today (RT) and the emerging Sputnik were still considered propaganda outlets set in place by Vladimir Putin, it was genuinely independent voices like Bausman, The Saker, analyst celebrities like Paul Craig Robert and Noam Chomsky, and even American patriots like Veterans Today editors Jim Dean and Gordon Duff, that tilted the balance then.

Russia Insider was the catalyst or a hub for transforming peace activism and fears for America-Russia tensions into a useful community and a meaningful voice of moderation. Articles scraped from all over the world carrying ideas and thought-provoking opinions were disseminated by a volunteer army that numbered in the dozens. There were so many RI activist volunteers, in fact, that neither Bausman nor I could figure out how best to utilize their talents and good will.

For the reader interested in discovering the mythical world of "Kremlin Tolls", Russia Insider was Pro-Russia central for many months after the MH17 provocation shocked the Russian Orthodox world awake. By February of 2015, my network included anyone that mattered in the spectrum of moderate Russia voices. As for Charles Bausman, while we did not always agree on strategies, there is no getting past how vital his role was in countering disastrous American policies and propaganda. It was Bausman who managed to support, via crowdfunding, a tiny independent resource capable of some degree of research.

By the time I met Charles Bausman, our company had lost fully half its PR business, and we had been forced to sell our most powerful media property Everything PR News to a New York PR guru. Russia Insider's reach and influence allowed Bausman to pay a few journalists, editors, and technical people to expand the site's reach. While this monetized aspect was not ultimately feasible for the long term, I and a few other team members could work more hours and harder to uncover news and to influence messaging.

While my stint at Russia Insider as publisher was short lived, articles conveying an alternative American view helped counterbalance overall Russophobic messages from the west to some degree.

"Blame it all on Putin all you want; the shrapnel tells no lies."

I recall one of my first pieces discussing the war in the Donbass was the story about a little boy blown literally to pieces by Poroshenko's artillery leveled onto Donetsk. Images of little Vanya still haunt me, and Graham Phillips brought the tale of Vanya Voronov to the forefront via his reporting and humanitarian efforts for the boy who lost two legs, one arm, and his vision to shrapnel. It's important to note here that hardly any western media carried Vanya's story even when Vladimir Putin saw to his hospital needs and made him a Russian citizen. Vanya's story, as captured on TV by Russia One's Irada Zeinalova, is a segment I cannot watch without weeping pitifully. Had the BBC and CBS covered this story in similar fashion Barack Obama would have had to call a halt to the Ukraine civil war immediately.

Returning to Russia Insider and Charles Bausman, I recall another aspect of his character that I learned about when he visited me here in Germany - his devout Orthodox Christianity, which I know powered much of his effort. Bausman has contributed a piece of his story for this book. My observations and participation in the Russian Insider endeavor will appear throughout the remainder of the book, but it will be Charles Bausman's notes that will best inform the reader about the development, import and future of independent media's role.

People are mad as hell - the story of Russia Insider

*"Every normal man must be tempted, at times,
to spit on his hands, hoist the black flag, and
begin slitting throats."*
– H.L. Mencken

A little over 2 years ago, while working in private equity investments in Moscow, Russia, specializing in agriculture, I started a small website, literally at my kitchen table. I thought it would be a little hobby, a place for me and a few friends to blow off some steam. Within a few months, with almost no investment, it had ballooned into a major media platform, one of the largest sources of news and analysis about Russia in the world.

We had stumbled on a gusher - a lot of pent-up anger in the US and Europe over how the truth about Russia was being trampled on by the media and politicians. The deception was extreme - and so was the reaction, and Russia Insider was at the center of it.

I was furious, as were many, about the dishonesty in the media about the Ukraine civil war. Living in Moscow and speaking fluent Russian, I was getting both sides of the story, and it was pretty obvious which side was lying. The anti-Russia bias in the media had long troubled us, but this pushed us over the edge.

This is a short account of the Russia Insider story, and what I think needs to happen to avert a grave threat to our very civilization.

The gusher

The hunger for news about Russia which contradicted the glaringly false narrative coming out of the media was insatiable. The more articles we published, the more our traffic grew - like wildfire. Yes, Russian official media - RT - had been doing something similar for about a decade, and doing it very well, but the deception and bias was so endemic and ingrained, and the need to correct it so dire, that the sector could - to this day - easily support a dozen like-minded outlets.

We were in the right place at the right time and quickly became the go-to and largest platform in the world (not counting RT) challenging what the media was saying about Russia.

In addition to the site, we started a Facebook page and Youtube channel, almost as an afterthought. Traffic on both also exploded. Within 18 months, across the site, social media, and Youtube, we were getting an average of 4 million visitors per month and 6 million views, and were regularly cited in the mainstream media. Counting republishing on other sites, our views approach 10 million per month. The demographics are interesting: 60% US and Canada, 35% Western Europe, 95% white male, mostly over 50, highly educated, high incomes.

Contributors, most of them volunteers, wrote original material, and in addition, we scanned the internet and reposted what we thought were the best articles about Russia, of which there turned out to be a huge number of excellent quality. Dozens of dissident analysts of the highest order had quietly emerged since the dawn of the blogosphere, and by curating what we thought were the best, and putting them in one place, we became essential reading for anyone following Russia, and a platform where many writers were glad to publish, because of the audience we could provide them.

In addition, we maintained a completely hands-off comment section, which we quickly realized was one of the biggest draws of the site. In short order, we ranked in the top 100 commenting sites in the world, ahead of heavyweights Newsweek, PBS, and Newsmax. Within our category, news and politics, we were in the top 50. In two years, we racked up over a million comments. But more important than their number was the quality and seriousness of many of them (yes there was also a lot of unpleasant abusive talk - inevitable in an unpoliced internet forum). It was always a source of amazement to us. A group of extremely well-informed regulars were routinely posting comments which often exceeded in length the articles they were discussing, and often with superb quality and insight.

It was a spontaneous and massive outpouring of talent and facts which were shredding the view of Russia pushed for decades in the mainstream media, along with the reputations of the 'commentariat' and their owners and editors doing the pushing. It was a popular insurrection against an effete and brittle elite trapped in their echo chambers, long since detached from reality. They never had a chance.

We are being censored

There is no question that traffic to Russia Insider is being partially blocked by the American government - by slowing the spread of our articles via Google, Twitter and Facebook, as confirmed by many other opposition media sources. On a level playing field our elites would be getting even more of a thrashing than they already are. Tipping the scales is one of the few moves they still have. But this too is unlikely to save them.

The fun

One of the most striking things to me about Russia Insider is how much fun it is. The Mencken quote above should be our corporate motto. We can't help ourselves, because the media and political figures we skewer make such deliciously rich targets of themselves. Like ridiculing the Catholic church in 1517, prospects are thick on the ground.

The permanently angry and prune-faced, stick-up-her-bum Anne Applebaum, the spidery Ed Lucas stalking the dark corridors of the Economist (we actually created a fake contributor named Russel O'Phobe with his picture), Rachel Maddow honking breathlessly about her latest blinding insight into the 'Russia Conspiracy', the frankly spooky

Masha Gessen looking for all the world like an evil dwarf out of a ghastly German fairy tale, Charles Krauthammer, who looks like his plastic surgeon was on a serious bender the day he mutilated him, the freakishly mean looking Samantha Power. The correlation between preaching lies, death and destruction, and looking evil goes way beyond coincidence.

The procession of spokes-buffoons at State and Pentagon were a comedian's gift and a stunning insight into the decline of a civilization. Jen Psaki, Marie Harf, and John Kirby will all always have a special place in my heart. You were truly remarkable, and thanks Nikki Haley for keeping the show going.

As soon as one hapless target exits stage left, our arrows protruding from it like some giant porcupine, another monstrosity heaves into view, begging for 'the treatment'. Our latest favorite is British former politician and journalist (she failed at both professions) Louise Mensch, reinvented as a social media maven and Russia conspiracy theorist, to whom the New York Times is happy to give prime placement on their op-ed page. The delusion and confusion about Russia is so deep, broad, and wide, that there is an almost endless supply of these characters. There are not enough hours in the day to do them all justice.

Note that the most egregious, the nastiest, the most hysterical offenders are mostly - women. There's a Sunday morning sermon in there somewhere, but that is a subject for a different essay.

Here are some examples of the humorous headline approach:

- "Ambitious Waffle House Bumpkin Nikki Haley Invents Her Own Middle East Policy"
- "Voice of America Tells the Truth about Ukraine, Hell Freezes Over"
- "John McCain's Latest Op-Ed More Brain Damaging Than Huffing Glue"

The talent

We frequently get emails from fans saying they are 'addicted' to the site, along with all manner of similar superlatives. One thing that made that possible was the extraordinary wealth of talent already writing about Russia in the blogosphere when we came along. We persuaded a large number of them to let us post their articles, and in a matter of months we had a better bench of analysts than any mainstream outlet could field, no matter how mighty. As we grew, more and more blogs and small sites were started, partially helped by the fact that we would carry their articles.

The writing was often superb, and the analysis solid. These were professors, businessmen, diplomats, journalists, investors, legal experts - experienced, serious professionals who often understood their subject and knew their facts far better than most journalists ever would. The typical profile; white men over 50 who had a little spare time on their hands. Put them in a head-to-head with your typical 20-

something being paid per click, or your ideologically blinkered striver at the Post or the Times, and it was no contest.

Another reason for the embarrassment of talent and knowledge was the degree to which media, government, and academia, had been hollowed-out by a strict insistence on a very dubious, neoconservative view which often stood in stark variance to the facts. That world was full of yes-men, neocon zealots, those willing to sacrifice principles to ambition, the intellectually lazy, and the just plain stupid - in short your typical modern journalist. It left out the better sort, and from this considerable population, a great many brilliant writers were born in the internet age.

When I first realized what was out there I was dumbfounded. They far outclassed the bench in the mainstream coming from the left and right and they had been shut out of the industry, and eager for a platform. A short list of a few names follows, to give you an idea. It is in no way complete, as there simply isn't enough room.

Some of the individuals:

Patrick Armstrong, Alex Mercouris, the Saker, Robert Parry, Ray McGovern, Peter Lavelle, Eric Kraus, Patrick Cockburn, John Pilger, Gil Doctorow, Stephen Cohen, Graham Phillips, Paul Robinson, Gordon Hahn, Ed Lozansky, Wayne Madsen, Anatoly Karlin, Giraldi, Paul Craig Roberts, Mark Ames, Michael Krieger, Justin Raimondo, Chris Hedges, Sharon

Tennison, James Carden, Phil Butler, Danielle Ryan, Anissa Naouai, Andrew Korybko, Mark Sleboda.

Some of the blogs:

South Front, Anti-media, Storm Clouds Gathering, The Blogmire, Antiwar.com, Counterpunch, Newsbud, The Intercept, Unz Review, Moon of Alabama, Kremlin Stooge, The Wall Will Fall, Off-Guardian, Signs of the Times, Global Research, American Committee for East-West Accord, Pravoslavie.ru.

And then, to add to all this wealth, in the summer of 2016 along came the Alt-Right, which to our surprise, packed a powerful intellectual punch along with a fascination and admiration for contemporary Russia and a blistering critique of neoconservatism. Some of their writing about the country is simply excellent. In particular Vincent Law and Richard Spencer.

Russian Christianity

Another story we realized was going almost completely unreported was the remarkable and dramatic turn towards Christianity at all levels of Russian society. Some of us, including myself, were practicing Russian Orthodox Christians, so it was very evident to us, and this topic also became a rich source of original material which was either ignored by the openly Christophobic mainstream, or crudely misreported as a negative.

One cannot remotely begin to understand Russia's past or present without understanding her nation-defining religion, and learning about it gave us extraordinary insight. The quantity of articles exceeded what we could put on Russia Insider, leading us to start a separate site - Russian Faith.

The remarkable Germans

On the subject of talent, the German blogosphere deserves special mention. I am half German, and so began to follow the German mainstream and alternative media, and was again amazed at what I discovered. It is hard to believe, but the German mainstream is more strident, brittle, and hysterically hostile towards Russia than even the Anglosphere.

Thankfully, Germans have demonstrated a healthy reaction to the nonsense, and they have a lively alt media scene, creating some of the best writing about Russia. We have carried many German articles in translation and continue to do so.

The crowdfunds

Russia Insider quickly outgrew my ability to fund it, so we embarked on a series of crowdfunds which brought in over $100,000 in the next 18 months. Readers also frequently simply hit the donate button, bringing in another $100,000. This is peanuts in the media world, but it was enough, together with ad revenue, for us to keep RI growing.

More than anything, it was yet more confirmation of a powerful, popular enthusiasm for what we were doing. We have received zero support from the Russian state. Everything we have done has been from contributions from thousands of individuals. It is a remarkable fact.

We really changed the debate

When we started in late 2014, what we were saying was shocking to many and definitely 'edgy'. But as Trump and Sanders emerged in late 2015 and early 2016, it felt like we were riding some sort of tsunami. I realized that we had been precursors to a massive popular revolt, that were being swept along by a vast crowd waking up to the corruption of their society. It was surreal to go from rabble-rousing outsiders to having both upstart candidates espousing some of our favorite talking points.

As I write this in June of 2017, the American political melt-down is the gift that keeps on giving, with Russia-gate pushing much of the American right into pro-Russian positions on Ukraine, Syria, and much else, which we were arguing two years ago, sending new audiences and admirers our way.

What needs to happen to make our media healthy again, and I've thought a lot about this, and what the prospects are for opposition media like Russia Insider.

The fact is that the media are by far the most important

political and social institution in society. They are more politically powerful than any branch of government, academia, or social or religious institution, especially in the apostate West. They literally tell people what to think on just about everything. Control the media and you control everything else - by default.

Watching and analyzing them as closely as I do, it is blindingly obvious to me that they are beyond repair - incapable of reform. The only solution is to replace them lock, stock and barrel with new outlets, new owners, new editors, and new writers, for the existing ones are incapable of change.

Only to the degree these new media appear can society address the crucial issues of our age. Nothing will improve until this is done - neither our endless wars, nor our political and social chaos. Any small progress we are making is thanks to the new media - whether on the right or the left.

Our media are our civilization's lifeblood, the mechanism by which it functions, and as long as they remain blindfolded, civilization not only cannot progress, but will regress and fail, as is clearly the case today.

For all our success, Russia Insider is relatively small, but taken together, the opposition media are formidable - they make up about 30% of the landscape in the US. They could well dominate relatively soon.

The funds required are not nearly what they used to be, for

new media is far cheaper than what was needed to build the legacy media. Perhaps a $1 billion of investment would be enough across the US market, a trivial sum on the national scale.

It's time for some patriotic and forward-thinking billionaires to step up to the plate and put some significant funds into this diverse crop of media upstarts like Russia Insider.

The truth about Russia

Russia is an incomparably fascinating, deep, wonderful civilization, one of the great world civilizations, with a fantastic wealth of ideas, culture, and Christian spirituality. The truth is that it is, and was, routinely smeared by its enemies, and its true nature is barely understood in the West.

It is like some priceless treasure, mothballed for the 20th century by Communism, and misconstrued before that. It has protected and defended at great cost the secrets and intellectual wealth inherited from the Byzantine empire, the most successful civilization man has ever known, going back to the very beginning of the Christian era. It is a veritable treasure chest now opening up to benefit all mankind.

The sole filter for information about Russia for decades have been the media, which have given a very slanted and frankly dishonest picture of the country - due to a bitter anti-Russian bias among its owners, editors and writers.

Actually, the deception goes back much further. It got started in late 18th c. England as Russia emerged as the British Empire's greatest global adversary. The deception was sustained by enlightenment, democratic, and liberal forces in Europe throughout the 18th and 19th centuries, whom Russia saw as mortal enemies, which they indeed turned out to be.

It is fair to say that the average Westerner, even the average highly-educated one, has a very faulty and slanted knowledge of Russia, tainted as it has been now for three centuries of outright hostility. I see it again and again when talking to highly educated and fair-minded people, especially older ones.

Perhaps we are on the cusp of a new era, when observers can write and think about Russia with a new eye, and begin to understand her majesty and promise, as Russia is only now beginning to do herself. She truly has much to offer the world, in knowledge, wisdom, and spirituality, like some vastly rich lost uncle we only recently became aware of.

There is a catastrophic shortage of Western writers who speak Russian well enough to really understand her. Amazingly, 90% of the people who write about her are more or less illiterate in her tongue, as are most Russians in English. This clearly needs to be overcome. There is a dangerous gap in communication, the harmful effects of which I observe on a daily basis.

Russia loves Russia Insider

The hearty enthusiasm which we met on a popular level is one of the fun distractions from the daily grind. Right-minded foreigners picking up shield and buckler and striking blows for Russia? - This can't help but warm the cockles of the Slavic heart.

The rollicking and popular political talk shows discovered us and as I speak Russian fluently enough, when in Russia, I sometimes go on, usually to explain the zany convulsions of American foreign policy.

As in the US, these shows feature top politicians, journalists, and academics, and it gives me a chance to meet and talk with them, and get insight into how they see the world, and their role in it. In this way, our team has access to some of the leading public personalities in Russia, sometimes forming strong friendships.

They often understand what is happening in the West far better than most Westerners. Their sources of information are excellent, and not hopelessly warped by the miasma of bias and deception Western policy-makers struggle under.

We were even awarded a prestigious Russian journalism prize, named after the Ukrainian author Oles Buzina. Accepting it was a truly humbling experience, borne as it was of the death and suffering of Ukrainian innocents on both sides.

Why we do this

Russia Insider continues to grow and deepen with each passing month. It is truly gratifying work, for it exposes lies and hypocrisy which wreak untold suffering around the world, not just in Russia.

We receive countless emails from readers with words to the effect that we have changed their life, struck the scales from their eyes, made them realize that a massive fraud and deception was being perpetrated, and how thankful they are to us.

It makes you want to get up in the morning and keep ramming the gates.

Charles Bausman

Chapter VI: Agents of Influence

As I suggested, my involvement with Russia Insider ratcheted up after a visit by Charles Bausman to my home in Germany. During that visit the RI founder and I had occasion to visit nearby Trier Cathedral (**Dom** St. Peter), where the seamless robe of Christ is enshrined. Bausman, who's devout Orthodox, was fascinated by this icon of faith as I recall. After our visit to the cathedral the Russia Insider founder asked me to help make use of volunteers attracted to the project, and to extend the social media, internet and political reach of the news outlet. Bausman, as an experienced Moscow businessman, had a "tiger by the tail" so to speak, for Russia

Insider served a growing community of people unwilling to accept the anti-Russia message. From its inception, Russia Insider was an alternative media hub, a source to turn to outside the mainstream and the propaganda of Radio Free Europe/Radio Free Liberty, the media weapons of the globalists.

One of the most important facets of my work with Bausman and associates was an increasing ability to tap the growing community of pro-Russia readers and journalists, to gather, filter, and distribute the other side of news and opinion about the Euromaidan coup d'etat in Ukraine and other topics. With western mainstream media operating in "parrot" mode, Russia Insider and other independent media became magnetic, attracting anyone interested in the dissenting view.

As for my role, I was the publisher of Russia Insider only in name. My real role was in evangelizing the platform, and in doing research needed to dig out the truth of critical stories. Russia Insider allowed contributors including me a lot more flexibility and freedom to look deep inside the extended network of actors in this new geopolitical drama unfolding. As a hub of media activity surrounding the anti-Russia issue, RI was a perfect vantage point from which to view the big picture. So, helping Russia Insider and using it to publish my own research was logical, as it was for other journalists who sought platforms outside the mainstream.

While MH17 dominated Russia Insider and most other pro-Russian media throughout the latter part of 2014, other crises would soon cause even more extensive independent media involvement, and Russia Insider offered an advantage for dissemination of the dissenting Russia view. As it turned out, the truth of matters concerning Russia would not have gotten as much traction without Russia Insider and the various collaborators with Bausman. So, when I appeared on RT to discuss the preposterousness of the western storyline on the Malaysian jet catastrophe, the focus was on the tabloid-like nature of media in the west.

The advantages of being an independent media outlet

became apparent very early on with the situation surrounding the so-called "Peacemaker Kill List," a website the Kiev fascists put up to reveal and target pro-Russian sympathizers. Russia Insider was one of the outlets breaking the story of the website in April 2015. This quote from one of the initial articles spells out the purpose of the "Peacemaker" web presence:

> *"The website publishes personal data about the traitors, separatists, supporters of the Russian invaders and the militants of illegal armed groups currently living in the temporarily occupied territory of Crimea (Ukraine)."*

Shortly after Russia Insider and other pro-Russian media broke the story of this "kill list", me and my small team set out to discover who was supporting such a dastardly effort to target anti-Maidan support in Ukraine. It did not take long to uncover the thinly veiled source of the effort. Sharing computer data, digital sources, and some social media profiling, we identified not only the persons behind the creation of the website and the domain, but we traced "Peacemaker" down to NATO servers via a series of fairly simple DOS commands like "tracert" (trace route). All this research revealed many of the people involved in the effort to target the Kiev government's opposition. We later traced those people back to the British Embassy in Ukraine, the German Foreign Ministry, and even the Ukraine OSCE through a loose connection with one of the perpetrators of the hit list. Many of the details were revealed in mine and

Holger Eekhof's article, *"What's Behind the "Peacekeeper" Killings in Ukraine?"*, which provided linkages deep inside the network the globalists are using to this day to undermine Russia and her relations with Ukraine.

One notable operative in all this, a lady named Nataliya Zubar had been instrumental in organizing the so-called "kill list" and an organization in Kharkov known as the Ukrainian Peacekeeping School, which was in turn funded by the British Embassy in Ukraine. We tracked Zubar down as the person who was, in fact, the technical director at Webby International Webhosting Inc. which had built and hosted the Peacemaker website. It's interesting to note that as recently as October 2016, Zubar is still involved in countering so-called Russian media aggression at this same agency. According to an article on Zubar's Maidan Monitoring Information Center (MMIC) has published in English recommendations for reform of Ukraine's international information and communication security, with the purpose of counter-propaganda against Russia. Maidan.org is essentially a tool of the Poroshenko regime in much the same way *Radio Free Europe*/Radio Free Liberty is a CIA and State Department arm of the US government.

Before I continue with the vital role Russia Insider played in countering US State Department messages, it is important to note how MMIC was and is still supported. A recent article by *Alex Christoforou at The Duran, and* republished at Zero Hedge details how George Soros was essentially in control of

Ukraine via NGO vehicles like the International Renaissance Foundation[13]. IRF is one of the listed support mechanisms for MMIC[14], which is in turn funded by a cadre of NGOs linked to; the Foreign and Common Wealth Office, U.K., the Polish Ministry of Foreign Affairs, the Czech Ministry of Foreign Affairs, and which can be easily connected to endeavors by British Petroleum (BP), Statoil, and other energy players[15].

The Ukraine-Euromaidan side of these media was manned by a vast and well-funded array of anti-Russia operators, countered on the Russian side by loosely organized and largely unfunded zealots. While RT and other Russian media vied for air time against the trillion-dollar western media behemoth, a few dozen so-called "Putin fans" interrupted the Euromaidan's revolutionary message. As the story continues, the reader will become better acquainted with the actors in this geopolitical drama. As a final note here, the role of the people and institutions mentioned in this "Peacekeeper" intrigue should be investigated by the appropriate tribunal, especially given the assassinations of Oles Buzina[16], and

---

[13]   Leaked Memo Proves Soros Ruled Ukraine In 2014: Minutes From "Breakfast With US Ambassador Pyatt" by *Alex Christoforou of The Duran*, Zero Hedge, August 20, 2016

[14]   Maidan Monitoring Information Center, World Maidan Organization website contacts page

[15]   Association of Middle East Studies (AMES) about page, Azeri Oil for Ukraine

[16] *Personal details of murdered journalist & ex-MP found posted on Ukrainian 'enemies of state' database*, RT, April 17, 2015

Donbass commanders Arseny Pavlov (callsign Motorola) and Mikhail Tolstykh (callsign Givi). For now, though, we need to return to Bausman's countermanding news outlet.

The role of Russia Insider as "Kremlin Troll Central," if you will, cannot be understated here. Within a few days of my "Peacekeeper" revelation, the Euromaidan agents began labeling me and a big swatch of independent voices with this derogatory name tag. From January to December of 2015 a Russophobe named Andrew Aaron Weisburd (@webradius) created a website dedicated to "Kremlin Trolls," which put me in the category, "entities with little or no deniability about relationships with the Russian Federation."

In other words, the people behind Euromaidan considered me, New Eastern Outlook, Graham Phillips, RT's Irish journalist Bryan McDonald and a few others number one enemies of the anti-Russia movement in Kiev. They even created an elaborate chart showing the loose connectivity in between alternative media, journalists, and embassies, etc.

For those of us identified on this chart and in diatribes at KremlinTrolls.com, being so named became a badge of honor. I'll never forget my fellow social media expert Marcel Sardo saying how exasperated he was when he learned that he was only classified as a "Basic Kremlin Troll" instead of as one of us "Putin Praetorians". In fairness to Sardo, the social media guru became one of the most vehement voices of dissent beginning, as I did, about the time of the Sochi Olympics. On his part, once again we find a common thread running through the pro-Russia activists. This quote from Sardo's contribution for this book is telling:

> *"Since I was familiar with the historical and socioeconomic ties Ukraine and Russia had since hundreds of years my concern about the consequences of this "uprise" grew by the day – especially when the first western politicians began parading on the Maidan unleashing their usual bullshit phrases about "western values", "freedom and democracy" "human rights". Everybody who observed the geopolitical events in the last 25, 30 years with open eyes and a waking mind knew that those hollow words are code-speak that will trigger a tragic bloodshed in one way or the other."*

Sardo will reveal more in his Kremlin Troll autobiography presently, but it's important for the reader to understand how the Euromaidan media and its megalithic western mainstream media support came into confrontation with an at first loosely knit group of Russia defenders. Sardo, like many of us, was "activated" by the unreal and often ludicrous messaging and imagery of the Kiev propagandists, and by the extremism of the Nazi Banderist thugs that were the shock troops of the illegitimate new Ukraine regime.

The separatists' plight in the east of Ukraine, the Odessa Massacre, the shelling of innocent civilians in the Donbass, and the one-sidedness of the western media galvanized natural opposition. My perspective on this polarization now reveals the breadth and diversity of the "troll army" Putin was supposed to have deployed. On the one hand, independent media and volunteer communities sprung up, and on the other end of the spectrum individuals in business and from the private sector took up the gauntlet.

Sardo, who has been featured in Swiss media as "Putin's media sniper," was born in Grenchen in the Canton of Solothurn, Switzerland. The son of Italian parents, this prominent pro-Russian evangelist is in business as a media producer creating various products for the film, television, internet and mobile telephony sectors. The following is his exclusive contribution to this volume you are reading.

Why I Stand with Russia by Marcel Sardo

I've been asked many times how I became part of the current information war, and why I stand with Russia. Here's part of my story.

I began visiting Russia regularly in 2006 at a time where the country still was recovering from the catastrophic 90's under then President Boris Yeltsin. Over the course, I observed carefully the first days of a new President named Vladimir Putin and took note of a certain progressiveness where

Moscow was concerned. Just four years into the Putin presidency, the Russian capital I often visited was in some aspect still a post-Soviet city, with lots of gray and dusty areas and remnants of the decay that beset the USSR.

Then in the following 11 years of my frequent visits, I could see the transformation of the country for the better. I experienced firsthand how public infrastructure improved, how people made it into a modest middle-class standard of living, and how the country steadily opened to become a Russian version of the west. I saw Russia adopting cultural items from the west, while at the same time converting them to fit into a Soviet shaped environment. One good example from my own industry was the Russian Music TV Channel RU.TV. On this channel, viewers could find 24 hours of music videos from all sorts of styles and genres invented in the west including Rock, R&B, Hip-Hop, Dance and Eurodance, Jazz, and more. Interestingly and appropriately, you will never encounter one music video in English on this channel. The whole 24 hours of broadcasts consist of Russian artists singing in the Russian language - but using western music genres. This self-awareness of the Russians and Russian society, along with various other personal experiences made me fall in love with the country. It was these experiences that led me to become a true friend of Russia and of the Russians.

Fast Forward to the year 2014, it was in mid-January 2014 that I returned to Switzerland from Saint Petersburg, where I had spent Christmas and New Year with Friends. This was the eve of the 2014 Sochi Winter Olympics and the beginning of a smear campaign against Russia using the so called "Sochi-Memes" and "Sochi-Fail." Having had quite a substantial experience with Russia and Russians, I knew that most of this allegation of those "failings" were fabricated and/or simply exaggerated. I instinctively jumped into the discussions on different readers forums of Swiss and German Newspapers and defended Sochi and Russia against these false allegations both by journalists and readers. At some point, I figured out that there was a huge debate happening on Twitter, and so I reactivated my old – virtually unused Twitter account, which barely had two dozen followers. It was now I began engaging via tweets too, and debating and fending off smears and lies surrounding the Sochi Olympics under the Hashtag #SochiFails. At this point, the whole online "battle" was a bit sportive and revolved around instances like the "Toilet-Compartments with two toilet seats." "Stray Dogs in the Media Center," "Missing Light Bulbs" and similar not-so serious problems of humanity. All in all, in retrospect, it was a funny short period where people banged on each other's heads with jokes and counter-jokes, fought a Meme with a Meme and a saucy insult with a digital middle finger. And then came the Maidan.

I experienced the outbreak and escalation of the Maidan mostly by sitting at my desk in my Zurich office and watching live streams from the Square on side monitors, while I worked. Since I was familiar with the historical and socioeconomic ties Ukraine and Russia had since hundreds of years, my concern about the consequences of this "uprising" grew by the day – and especially when the first western politicians began parading on the square unleashing their usual bullshit phrases about "western values", "freedom and democracy" and preaching "human rights". Everybody who has observed the geopolitical events in the last 25, 30 years with open eyes knows that those hollow words are code-speak that often trigger terrible bloodshed in one way or the other. After all, who among us can forget the "humanitarian bombing" of Yugoslavia, the "liberation of Iraq" from a "brutal dictator" and the eternal happiness, freedom, and prosperity that subsequently came upon the Iraqi population? And of course, the pinnacle success of nation building in Libya after imposing a "no fly zone" over that country, which magically turned into an "only NATO fly zone," is a lesson in exported democracy for all. The coup that was to ensure "fundamental human rights" for the Libyan people – was burned into history just as Gaddafi got sodomized to death in front of running cameras. But what alarmed me most on the Maidan was the fact the coverage of events in the western mainstream media never corresponded with what I was watching on various Live-Streams or what I was reading on myriad independent forums and blogs from Ukraine and Russia. It was here it dawned in me that this was the perfect moment to stage a mass deception of the western audience over the events in Ukraine (or rather in Kiew) by those in control of the Western mainstream media. Simply by using the advantage of the language barrier, most people in the west would be unable to consult primary sources or to get first-hand reports. So, people in North America and Europe proper could only rely on what their media was reporting. In this way, the media in cahoots with the forces behind Maidan for their "truth" on the matter. As it happened, westerners were never informed about grassroots resistance to the Maidan uprisings, so viewers thought "the whole of Ukraine" was in rebellion. (Thus, the often-used phrase: "The people of Ukraine made their choice"...). In this way, the language gap was to become the wide-open backdoor that allowed the contravening forces in the west to spin and disseminate the desired narrative and to spread it almost uncontradicted to westerners. Enter the strength of blogging desperados.

When the Maidan reached its climax in February 2014 the western propaganda gates were flung wide open, and the cooperate, and government media from the west flooded the airwaves with half-truths, distortions and straight out lies. A sticky spider's web of false narratives was spun out over the brains of the public in the west: Crimea was "invaded," "Terrorists occupied" the Donbas, and the Attack of the Ukrainian Army on its own population was rebranded as an "anti-Terror Operation." Scores of Videos emerged from down on the ground, stories of atrocities (The Korsun Massacre) and crimes against the population of Donbass were reported in Russian and Ukrainian blogs too – and everything was well documented in words, pictures and videos - but all this was conveniently ignored by western

MSM or decried as "Russian Propaganda" one. This was the moment when I decided to get involved and to do something. As a media producer myself, I figured out the best way I could serve the truth would be to engage in confronting the media and in breaking the silence. In short, I decided to do what I can do best, to propagate the other side of the story. Together with Gleb Bazov and 3 other social media activists, I created a blog named slavyangrad.org where we would engage in translating blog entries and videos from the battle zones provided by the Russian and Ukrainian side into English, Spanish, and German. Though we were a small voice in a vast sea of worldwide media messages, we did serve as one small force of resistance against the unified wall of silence and lies that was set up by the established Western media.

Enthusiasm was great at the beginning, none of us got paid, and most of us invested all their free time in this venture. We created blogs, YouTube channels, we created Skype Chat Groups where we exchanged information and coordinated translation, and we engaged in readers forums and comment sections to post our resources and fight against the general propagated narrative spread by the corporate media. As the western narrative more and more became a tool in the hands of the globalists and NATO, we were shocked to discover we were one of the only sources to have created a space where the other side of the events could be published and distributed. People like KAZZURA who translated and subtitled scores of videos from the battle fields in Donbas emerged out of nothing. Collectives like VOX POPULI EVO or SOUTHFRONT, DONI News, individuals like Graham Phillips and others who reported directly from the ground led the truth narrative from Donbass. For whatever reason and motivation all these people and collectives engaged in what they were doing – they were doing because they wanted to give those in the Donbass a voice, and the right to be heard – a right that was taken away from them by the forces of evil who have taken over the corporate media under their control and turned it into a tool of mass deception. We all knew we are on the right side of history. We all knew we were doing the right thing. I will look back to this time of my life as the time of awakening from lifelong slumber where I allowed the corporate media and established normalcy to delude me with their lies. It was the time when I liberated myself from being fed the news, and the time I learned how to search for the truth. This was the radicalizing effect of the #OdessaMassacre.

Marcel Sardo, Pro-Russia Media-Sniper

Once again, the now familiar thread of sincere indignation as the cause of activism is evident. Marcel Sardo, like other pro-Russian voices mentioned so far, entered the political fray because of the imbalance and the untruths. All throughout my experiences in the ranks of alleged Kremlin puppets, I've found this thread of incredulity and reflexive resistance to the injustices heaped upon the Russians. Right or wrong, the clear bias in reporting news from Ukraine served the Russian cause better than any state-owned media or diplomat.

It is in overlooking this facet of the 21st century variant of the Great Game that the globalists made a grievous miscalculation. The digital and social media cyberwar we see waged now has been almost a total loss for the western mainstream. Sardo's part, my role, and the efforts of the rest of the alleged Kremlin cyber agents will be highlighted all throughout this volume. However, the success of my Kremlin Troll comrades can easily be seen in the latest efforts in Germany and the EU, with the neocons and the technocrats in ramping up social media censorship on a massive scale. While traditional media like the New York Times and the Washington Post, and broadcast news channels such as BBC and CNN, were easily leveraged by billionaire owners, social media like Facebook and Twitter were discounted by the aging elites.

Another critical voice, Patrick Armstrong, added credibility and pragmatic correctness that Russia Insider and the "message" needed. As anyone who has toyed with social media knows, sarcasm and the pseudo-intellectual game are played in heated intensity. Underneath though, in the stories and reports needed to properly drive a real message, real research and moral character sent Putin's stock higher. With regard to Armstrong, I recall the article that brought his intellectual voice to my attention. Published on Russia Insider in April 2015, his article "The West Throws a Temper Tantrum" was a template for the deconstruction of the blasphemous NATO troll lie. In the report, Armstrong levels Graham's useful hierarchy of disagreement against the idiotic arguments that "trolls" hollering "liar, liar, pants on fire" will ever change the mind of someone with a different idea or view. Armstrong's "proof," as it were, is part of the basis for this book. For the same reason Vladimir Putin has little need of billions in personal wealth, the Russian leadership never deployed any such useless army of idiots.

Armstrong, a well-respected and long serving analyst of first the Soviet Union and later Russia, is a brilliant if somewhat austere colleague who has given a lot to the positive discussion of Russia. Here's a short autobiographical sketch by Dr. Armstrong and his contribution about a huge lost opportunity cost that few understand.

The Confession of Patrick Armstrong

I started work for the Canadian Department of National Defense in 1977 in the Directorate of Land Operational Research of the Operational Research and Analysis Establishment. I participated in many training games in real time and research games in very slow time. The scenarios were always the same: we (Canada had a brigade group in West Germany) were defending against an attack by the Soviet/Warsaw Pact side. In those days NATO was a defensive organization and, as we later found out, so was the other side: each was awaiting the other to attack. Which, come to think of it, is probably why we're all here today.

I enjoyed my six years, often as the only civilian in a sea of uniforms, but I realized that a history Ph.D. stood no chance of running the directorate so, when the slot opened, I contrived to switch to the Directorate of Strategic Analysis as the USSR guy. I should say straight off that I have never taken a university course on Russia or the USSR. And, in retrospect, I think that was fortunate because in much of the English-speaking world the field seems to be dominated by Balts, Poles or Ukrainians who hate Russia. So, I avoided that "Russians are the enemy, whatever flag they fly" indoctrination: I always thought the Russians were just as much the victims of the ideology as anyone else and am amused how the others have airbrushed their Bolsheviks out of their pictures just as determinedly as Stalin removed "*unpersons*" from his.

That was November 1984 and Chernenko was GenSek and, when he died in March 1985, Gorbachev succeeded. While I didn't think the USSR was all that healthy or successful an enterprise, I did expect it to last a lot longer and when Gorbachev started talking about glasnost and perestroika, I thought back to the 20th Party Congress, the Lieberman reforms, Andropov's reforms and didn't expect much.

In 1987 two things made me think again. I attended a Wilton Park conference (the first of many) attended by Dr. Leonid Abalkin. He took the discussion over and, with the patient interpretation of someone from the Embassy, talked for hours. The Soviet economy was a failure and couldn't be reformed. *That* was something different. Then, on the front page of Pravda, appeared a short essay with the title "A New Philosophy of Foreign Policy" by Yevgeniy Primakov. I pricked up my ears: a *new* philosophy? But surely good old Marxism-Leninism is valid for all times and places. As I read on, I realized that this was also something new: the author was bluntly saying that Soviet foreign policy had been a failure, it was ruining the country and creating enemies. These two were telling us that *the USSR just didn't work*. As Putin told Stone, "it was not efficient at its roots."

These things convinced me that real change was being attempted. Not just fiddling around at the edges but something that would end the whole Marxist-Leninist construct. As far as I was concerned, it had been the communist system that was our enemy and, if it was thrown off, we should be happy. Sometime around then I was interviewed for a job at NATO, and the question was what, with all these changes, was NATO's future. I said it should become an alliance of the civilized countries against whatever dangers were out there: the present members of course, but also the USSR, Japan and so on.

Well, that didn't happen, did it? I remember a very knowledgeable boss assuring me that NATO expansion was such a stupid idea that it would never happen. He was wrong too.

In 1814 the victors – Britain, Russia, Prussia, and Austria – sat down in Vienna, with France, to re-design the world. They were wise enough to understand that a settlement that excluded France wouldn't last. In 1919 this was forgotten and the settlement – and short-lived it was – excluded the loser. In 1945 Japan and Germany were included in the winners' circle. At the end of the Cold War, repeating the Versailles mistake, we excluded Russia. It was soon obvious, whatever meretricious platitudes stumbled from the lips of wooden-faced stooges that NATO was an anti-Russia organization of the "winners."

But I retained hope. I think my most reprinted piece has been "*The Third Turn*" of November 2010 and in it I argued that Russia had passed through two periods in the Western imagination: first as the Little Brother then as the Assertive Enemy but that we were now approaching a time in which it would be a normal country.

Well, that didn't happen, did it?

And so, the great opportunity to integrate Russia into the winners' circle was thrown away.

For a long time, I thought it was stupidity and ignorance. I knew the implacably hostile were out there: Brzezinski and the legions of "think" tanks (my website has a collection of anti-Russia quotations I've collected over the years) but I greatly underestimated their persistence. Stupidity and ignorance; you can argue with those (or hope to). But you can't argue with the anti-Russians. Russia wants to reconquer the empire, so it invaded Georgia. But it didn't hold on to it, did it? No, but that's because we stopped it. Putin kills reporters. Name one. You know, whatshername. There were provocative exercises on NATO's borders. But NATO kept moving closer to Russia. Irrelevant, NATO's peaceful. Putin is the richest thief in the world. Says who? Everybody. Putin hacked the US election. How? Somehow.

I quoted Hanlan's razor a lot — "never attribute to malice that which is adequately explained by stupidity." And, stupidity and ignorance they were — a favorite being John McCain's notion that the appropriate venue for a response to a Putin piece in the NYT was Pravda. And then he picked the wrong Pravda! But he won't hate Russia or Putin any the less if he were told that, would he?) At some point, I came to understand that *malice* was the real driver.

I suppose it grew on me bit by bit — all the stupidity converged on the same point, and it never stopped, but real stupidity and ignorance don't work that way: people learn, however slowly. I think the change for me was Libya. I started out thinking stupidity but, as it piled up, it became apparent that it was malice. I'd seen lies in the Kosovo war but it was Libya that convinced me that it wasn't just *a few* lies, it was *all* lies. My guess is that Libya was a significant development in Putin's view of NATO/US too.

Naive perhaps but, for most of history, stupidity has adequately explained things and malice is, after all, a species of stupidity.

So, what's the point of writing? I'll never convince the Russia haters, and there's little chance of getting through to the stupid and ignorant. And most people aren't very interested anyway.

Well, this is where malice meets stupidity. If we consider the *Project for a New American Century*, the neocon game plan "to promote American global leadership," what do we see twenty years later? Brzezinski laid out the strategy in *The Grand Chessboard* at the same time. What today? Well, last year he had to admit that the "era" of US dominance, he was so confident of twenty years earlier, was over. There's no need to belabor the point: while the US by most measures is still the world's dominant power, its mighty military is defeated everywhere and doesn't realize it, its manufacturing capacity has been mostly outsourced to China, domestic politics and stability degenerate while we watch and there's opioids, spectacular debt levels, incarceration, infant mortality, недоговороспособны and on and on. Donald Trump was elected on the promise to Make America Great... *Again*. Hardly the hyperpower to lead the Globe, is it?

The Twentieth Century was the "American Century" thanks to unlimited manufacturing capacity allied to great inventiveness anchored on a stable political base. What is left of these three in 2017? *Can* America be made "great" again? And wars: wars everywhere and everywhere the same. And what other than *malice* has brought it to this state? Malice has become stupidity: the neocons, Brzezinskis, the Russia haters, the "*Exceptionalists*," scheming "to promote American global leadership," have weakened the USA. Perhaps irreparably.

So, who's the audience today? The converted and people at the point when a little push can break their conditioning have always been there. But now there is a potentially huge audience for our efforts: *the audience of the awakening*.

Which brings me back to where I started. Except that it's the USA this time: *IT'S NOT WORKING!*

We're here, and we're waiting for you: you've been lied to, but that doesn't mean that everything is a lie.

Patrick Armstrong

Chapter VII: Kremlin Birdwatchers[17]

I'll never forget the first time I watched Graham Phillips broadcasting from Ukraine. The British journalist and videographer had already been living in the country for some time, and cataloging everything from concerts to travel experiences when the Euromaidan protests erupted. Phillips was one of those present in Maidan Square when Ukraine turned upside down, and across the revolutionary front from Donbass to Crimea. I first caught sight of him working with RT for Sloviansk in April 2014 at the onset of hostilities in between the Kiev regime and the pro-Russian separatists. I recall Phillips broadcasting without a helmet or flak vest, from inside a burned-out transport with a giant rocket hole in its side. I also remember thinking at the time, "Okay, this guy won't be alive long once the shrapnel starts flying." Clearly, I was wrong. Phillips did survive, and he became a sort of urban legend for his brash war-front encounters and for his bravado standing among the fierce Donbass militiamen fighting off Ukraine regulars.

At the time, I had no idea Graham and I would become friends. Then later that same year Graham was captured at

---

[17]   Birdwatcher - slang term used by British Intelligence for a spy

Donetsk Airport by the UKROPS. Fans of his video reports and his Twitter feed went frantic, fearful the Nazi right wing of Ukraine would surely kill the British journalist for what they would allege – but knew was really not - Russian propaganda against them. I came to Graham's aid as well, and publicly warned the illegitimate Kiev regime leadership and its US enablers of the massive backlash they would incur should Phillips come to harm. Interrogated, somewhat abused and ultimately banished from Ukraine, Graham lived to tell the tale that no other journalists, especially the western media, seemed able to tell at the time.

Deeply embedded with the pro-Russia forces of Donbass, Phillips showed the willing world a real war correspondent's view of the civil conflict. RT eventually dropped Phillips' coverage for yet undisclosed reasons, but the broadcasts continued with the aid of photojournalist Patrick Lancaster. Phillips reported while taking cover from fire at the Donetsk Airport, from Crimea and Odessa, and even at DPR cookouts with Donbass heroes. For the UKROPS (Ukrainian Association of Patriots or Nazis), people like this would certainly be labeled "birdwatchers" in spy slang.

For me, Graham is a friend and an example. He is an ordinary person who took on an extraordinary responsibility. I watched his cataloging of the utter catastrophe that Ukraine became. Phillips walked side-by-side with Donbass heroes Motorola (Arsen Sergeyevich Pavlov) and Givi (Mikhail Sergeyevich Tolstykh), and with my "brat" (brother) Russell

"Texas" Bonner Bentley, who will also be profiled here.

Phillips delivers perhaps the best example of fearless journalism covering the Ukraine uprising. Here is his story as a Kremlin Troll, told in his own words.

Graham Phillips

When Euromaidan got going, I was living in Odessa, in the south of Ukraine. Before this, from 2011 to the start of 2013, I had lived in Kiev. It was during this span I first noticed a change in the political situation of the country.

After the October 2012 elections, this was when the neo-Nazi party Svoboda captured around 10% of the vote, some seats in parliament, and when the almost daily disorder began. Svoboda started using their ballot boost, fueled by a general turn to ultra-nationalism, to ramp up their ultra-nationalist, far-right program. Their strategies included regular protests, coordinated attacks on events, aggression toward people not fitting their agendas, and a high-octane Congress in as of December 2012. It was via my capacity as a freelance journalist that I first covered all these events and more. So, from the start of Maidan, seeing the people I'd covered in Kiev, such as Svoboda, behind it, I knew that nothing good would come of it.

I liked Ukraine, the country as it was - far from perfect, however, it was a country, had its charm, people got on. I'd created a life there, purchased an apartment in Odessa even From Odessa, watching Maidan begin filled me with a sense of foreboding. More, a sense of wrong being perpetrated, as looking at Maidan coverage in western media, all there was, was blanket pro-Euromaidan coverage.

Working as a freelance journalist in Odessa as I was - although to take into account that there was less news there than Kiev, hence less earnings, and also that I was working on longer, book projects, I'd also built up a business as an English corporate teacher - I began actively writing posts on my blog on the side of Maidan I saw wasn't being covered by the west In December of 2013, I was surprised to get a message on Facebook from a producer at the channel Russia Today, inviting me on air for an interview.

I've never thought of working with Russian media, but, from Odessa, I did the interview, and my relationship with RT began.

By this time, I'd already started doing some of my own filming, just picking up my camcorder, and going with it. And things went from there. I was doing my own recording, travelling all around the then east of Ukraine, and Crimea, also interviews for RT. In April, RT asked me to go to Donetsk for a week of work, so I left my home in Odessa, and it all began. My relationship with RT ended in July of 2014, after my 2nd deportation, and I worked for a bit for Russian channel Zvezda, but for some 2 and a half years now, I've been working entirely for myself. I've covered extreme war in Donbass, from battles at Donetsk airport, Debaltsevo, to daily shelling of Lugansk, where I lived under blockade for a month, in 2014. I've filmed civilians killed by Ukrainian shelling, on a daily basis, Donetsk, January 2015. MH17. It's not something I could ever have expected would happen in my life, nor in a country, as it was Ukraine, where I moved, liked, and just expected a positive new experience in life from. However, it's happened, and I've stayed with it, and will stay with it till the end. At all times, I've done my best, always reported things as they are, the reality of the situation, fought propaganda where I've seen it, brought the truth out of Donbass, and the real situation there.

Graham Phillips

The positive and negative energy in flux around the whole Russia issue served to elevate me and several others to the top position among so-called Kremlin Trolls. As I alluded to earlier, the pressure I applied about MH17 and the "kill list" stories really infuriated Euromaidan Press and the whole of the opposition. In a funny twist of fates, the site dedicated to us Putin fans, kremlintrolls.com lowered the status of the top three original Kremlin Trolls, my comrades; Marcel Sardo, malinka1102 (Malinka), and @mkj1951 (Marilyn Justice) to "ordinary trolls", and elevated me, Graham Phillips, RT's Mark Sleboda and Dmitry Zolotarev, and a few others up there with the outlets Sputnik UK, New Eastern Outlook, and even the Russian Embassy in Ottowa(?) to the pinnacle of Rusky propagandists.

Created by the notorious founder and director of Internet Haganah, and of the Society for Internet Research, Andrew Aaron Weisburd, kremlintrolls.com was intended to serve in the same ways the anti-Islam Haganah (Zionist for the early Israel Defense Forces) was leveraged to defame anybody remotely against Israel's policies. While Internet Haganah operated from Weisburd's home office under the guise of an internet anti-extremist security league, my suspicions are that he's more likely a freelancer and functionary of the Israeli and probably the US intelligence community. His LinkedIn profile reveals recommendations from West Point graduates like *Robert A. Fox, who's a* fellow in the Foreign Policy Research Institute's Program on the Middle East as well as a Senior Fellow at the Center for Cyber and Homeland Security at The George Washington University. Fox *was an* FBI Special Agent on a Joint Terrorism Task Force (JTTF) and Executive Officer of the Combating Terrorism Center at West Point (CTC), and he recommended Weisburd for intelligence analysis alongside other quasi-spooks offering accolades. The "rabbit hole" on Weisburd is deep and dark, but his Kremlin Troll charts prompted New York Times political writer Scott Shane to request an interview with Malinka when she was a top three troll. At this point it's appropriate for me to introduce the person behind the "Malinka" twitter feed, a lady whose witty grandmother disguise demands that I withhold her real name to protect she, her husband, their children and grandchildren from the people who create "kill lists" targeting Putin fans.

Letter from Malinka1102: Putin Twitter Spy

When you asked me how I got into this whole anti-Russia

affair, I tried to remember how I've got into twitter life in the first place. I recall opening my account a long time ago but not having even used it much until 2014. I remember I used to watch BBC, Channel 4, read The Guardian for news and had my favorite journos there. Then the Ukraine, Crimea, and anti-Russia events started. It was then I noticed something is was not quite right, the information from UK news and from Russia was very different.

Since I have a lot of friends in Russia, and since I go there every year, I also had firsthand knowledge and reactions to events from Russians. So, naturally, I wanted to get all possible info from different sources to make up my own mind on these important developments. That's how I got became a kind of twitter aficionado. It did not take long for me to realize that UK media (and western MSM in general) were propagating their own anti-Russia narrative, the very same journos, who I had great respect for, were very biased and the often-twisting facts to fit a clear agenda. So then and now I check different anti- and pro-Russian sources on the same subject, including the quotes and etcetera, before tweeting.

I've been blocked by many officials and journos just for asking questions or confronting them with facts from western media (to avoid being accused of citing Russian sources [which equal] as they say, "propaganda") Also, as you probably know, I'm on the list of "Top Kremlin Trolls". I've been challenged a few times to reveal my [identity and] personal [information] to prove I'm not a troll (@FactCheck and one NYT journo in DM). But I declined those requests since it doesn't matter who I am. It seems apparent to me that what is really important is what I say. So, it is with a clear conscience I can tell the media or anyone: "No, I'm not paid by anyone, I have no connections with Russian government or secret services."

@Malinka1102

My own relationship with Malinka came about in the most natural way. Despite what is often claimed about Vladimir Putin taking over social media I can tell you this, the Russians don't know any more about Twitter and Facebook than the Americans or Germans do. You "follow" somebody on Twitter because they follow you or "like" you and vice-versa. Malinka retweeted some article of mine, or I liked or retweeted some information she found. This is the way of social media. Even though social media experts can profile accounts like I've done for reports and stories, in general, your following is made up of people following the same message you do.

Malinka first retweeted and followed me over a post on my personal blog back in December of 2014 in which I profiled some of the real NATO agents and their trolling activities. I recall this time when the Kiev Post's Christopher Miller was just building up his reputation as a US State Department anchorman in Kiev. Miller would later go on to work with my old friend Pete Cashmore's Mashable (as a kind of reward for Russophobia), but he and the now notorious Eliot Higgins (aka Bellingcat) got their start battling ordinary people like Malinka on Twitter. I'm now blocked from seeing Miller's tweets, which is interesting since I'm unaware of anyone else in the world blocking me.

I mention Miller for one reason. While Vladimir Putin's alleged plans for world domination apparently lean heavily on ordinary people, the anti-Russia side is mainly comprised of western media types who were supported and advanced by what is commonly referred to in the Trump era as the "deep state". At this point, I can name many western "spooks" who took up the banner of the Obama administration's war on Putin. However, one interesting fellow that comes to mind is Dr. John R. Schindler, who is a former professor at the US Naval War College and intelligence analyst and counterintelligence officer for the NSA. He's got upwards of 240,000 Twitter followers (half appear to be bought), and he calls people I know "Kremlin Troll".

However else I gauge Schindler's expertise on who is or is not a Kremlin Troll, his resignation from the US Naval War College[18] over allegations he shared pictures of his sex organs on Twitter spoiled my further investigations into his NSA Troll efforts forever. I'll refrain from saying more on this, but an article by Schindler on his XX Committee blog[19] entitled "When Kremlin Trolls Attack" bears scrutiny here. The piece begins with polemical sophisty:

> *"The reality that Russia buys, or at least rents, trolls by the battalion to harass, intimidate and make life unpleasant for anybody who opposes Moscow policy, while employing aggressive agitprop to further Putinist propaganda, isn't exactly news, but it's nevertheless welcome to*

---

[18]   U.S. Naval War College professor resigns after probe into lewd photo found online, New York Daily News, August 12, 2014 via News Wire Services

[19]   When Kremlin Trolls Attack, The XX Committee, February 23, 2015

see mainstream outlets doing some digging into what's going on."

Schindler at once embellishes himself as a leader of the anti-Snowden cadre of NSA counterintelligence supporters, while at the same time playing the poor and pitiful blogger that mighty Vladimir Putin ordered his troll armies to crush. The former Naval War College professor even went so far as to accuse Russia Insider of deploying "active measures" against him. Schindler is an insignificant player in all this new Cold War mess, but these grandiose traits are, for me, symptomatic of anti-Russia pundits out there. Another name that comes to mind is Newsweek's Kurt Eichenwald, who seems to alternate between being a confidant of deep state intelligence agencies and the victim of secret Kremlin troll measures to make opposition reporters have seizures[20].

The social media landscape is littered with the virtual corpses of NATO and corporate media minions who thought they were prepared to do battle in the digital world. As somebody who's been descended upon by the best internet search and hacker trolls in the business, I can honestly call these people crybabies too thin-skinned to even give social media a decent go. A final note on the man who created the ubiquitous Kremlin Troll "proofs," A. A. Weisburd spent hundreds of hours comparing Twitter connections only to end up like just any other finger pointing globalist pawn. On

---

[20]   Newsweek's Kurt Eichenwald Claims Twitter Troll Gave Him Seizure, Taking Social Media Hiatus, Alex Griswold, Mediaite, December 16, 2016

"strategies" Putin is supposed to employ, Weisburd listed[21] every US State Department or NATO instruction for propaganda, like so:

> *"The eighth method is finding the scapegoat. In the Ukraine, the scapegoat is the Right Sector, oligarchs, Russia is also allegedly harmed by the West by sticking their nose everywhere."*

At the end of the book I will attempt to list most of the dutiful Kremlin Trolls, but for now, I must recall my interactions with them chronologically. From early 2015 my RT and Russia Insider contributions led to me being introduced to maybe the most fascinating or all "Putin fans," an American engineer named Eric C. Anderson who currently lives in Manaus, at the confluence of the Rio Solimões and the Rio Negro, at the upper Amazon River, of all places.

If ever the mighty reach and influence of Vladimir Putin were in question, Kremlin Trolls in Amazonas speaks to this issue. Eric is my friend since our first encounters on Facebook, a humble man whose life has been an almost incredible adventure. Throughout a hundred or more conversation with Eric, I have been continually surprised at the Hollywood-like character he presents. Wearing his straw planter's hat, the 6'-6" Anderson reminds one of a character from a film like Indiana Jones or perhaps a rugged Bogart in *Treasure of the Sierra Madre.*

With the epic Amazonas backdrop floating past his aluminum johnboat[22], the former software engineer is evidence that Putin's infamous "troll army" is far more complex than any western propagandist or NATO analyst ever could imagine. The Virginia native who spent most of his adult life in Washington DC spends his retirement these days giving guided tours to Amazon nature researchers. What Eric does best though, besides gathering intelligence for Putin on the Amazon's rare Hyacinth Macaw[23], is living and experiencing. Besides being a top secret operative of the Kremlin embedded deep in the middle of nowhere, Eric divides his time between solitary exploring all along the upper Amazon by boat and enjoying time with the locals in remote Manaus, which is a city that preserves the habits of native Brazilian tribes.

---

[22]   Johnboat definition, "a narrow flat-bottomed square-ended boat usually propelled by a pole or paddle and used on inland waterways", Merriam-Webster

[23]   Hyacinth Macaw (Anodorhynchus hyacinthinus), a bird species native to central and eastern South America and are listed as "vulnerable" by IUCN, Audubon Nature Institute.

How I Became a Putin Troll and Kremlin Puppet by Eric C. Anderson

My journey into the pro-Russia camp was about unlearning

American propaganda.

In some respects, I was always a very typical American. I was a workaholic who constantly stressed out over my projects. I was continually trying to stay up to date in my field of computer software, I also worried about my marriages, and I suffered from stress-related illnesses. Socially, I wanted people to think I was up-to-date, so I read the Washington Post and listened to NPR every day. Added to all this "so typical" attitude, I I wanted distraction and excitement, so I traveled at every opportunity. Computer programming is project-oriented, so I would just finish a project and go.

If imagery serves the reader, I was more Forrest Gump than a sexy investigative journalist, but I wanted to have adventures and to travel, and the more adventurous, the better. I hitchhiked to Mexico and Guatemala in 1983. Then I met a Syrian girl in Washington, married her in Damascus in 1984, backpacked with her around Jordan, Turkey, and Egypt. I even found myself in Haiti n 1987 for a while, later hiking it all around South America. It was then I saw the Amazon river for the first time in 1986 and moved here to Brazil in 1992. Divorced from my first wife, I married a local girl and bounced in between America and Manaus Brazil until retiring a few years ago.

Then when Bush and his cronies stampeded us into war in 2003, I had had enough. I joined the marches in the streets of Washington and New York. During this time, I learned to recognize the neocons, and I found out about the powerful influence of the Israel lobby. I asked myself and my contemporaries the question; "It they were lying about Iraq, what else were they lying about?" I wonder to this day what lies I probably still have rattling around in my skull.

Then the internet exploded. NOW anyone can look stuff up and figure things out. But what about Russia specifically? After 1991, Russia dropped out of my limited field of vision. The evil USSR was gone. End of story.

Then Naomi Klein's 2007 *Shock Doctrine* had a chapter about the pillage of Russia after the Yeltsin years. "Damn," I had thought Yeltsin was a hero, but this revelation changed my mind.

Then in August of 2008, I was falling asleep watching the TV news laying next to my Russian girlfriend in my Washington flat. On the news, missiles were flying around in an obscure place called Georgia. The only message of the broadcasts was "The evil Putin Is Invading." Whatever was indeed happening was important, but these were the same newscasters were who lied us into Iraq. I at first figured the Georgia conflict was about the oil pipeline but learned later there were far bigger wheels turning.

My Russian girlfriend never talked about geopolitics, so I had not the slightest idea how she felt about Putin until I drew her out in 2011. She liked Putin just fine, but don't share that with our Ukie friends. I was mystified, as I had a hard time telling the difference between our Ukie and Russian friends.

Next, the Sochi Olympics came, and the anti-Russian propaganda was thick. There was Victoria Nuland's smirking face on my TV screen and all over the internet, and since by that time I knew damn well who the neocons were, their bringing yet another war was readily apparent. But I was still mystified at their hostility toward Russia. In February 2014, I was back in Brazil and following the Maidan Coup on the internet. The neocon lies were thick, and it was so apparent for me this was a USA-backed coup. I also knew that if the neocons were involved, then surely there was an Israel component.

The Odessa Massacre of May 2014 and the memes of Colorado beetles, patterned like St George Ribbons, being burned by cigarette lighters – the message was clear the Americans, and their allies were trying to provoke Putin into an impetuous response. And anger is a powerful motivator.

After Odessa, matters only got worse. First, the MH17 tragedy and the massive American propaganda. Then the suspicious Sinai plane crash and the knowledge my Russian friend takes that flight sometimes. A blatantly obvious false flag in Syria in 2013 and the aftermath of Russia's whole fight against terrorism versus the USA pretending to fight terrorism while overthrowing Syria for Israel and a pipeline – all this and much more let me have nothing but contempt for the American media and our government spokesmen. They insulted our intelligence, and Russian media like RT left me feeling more informed, thereby gaining my trust.

So, this is how I suppose "Kremlin Trolls" are converted, if you ask me. By telling the more reasonable truth and by gaining trust.

Eric C. Anderson

Chapter VIII: Putin's Provocateurs

"Europeans are really dying out!"
Vladimir Putin

In Russian spy terminology provocateurs are operatives sent to incite a target group to action for entrapping or embarrassing them. Clearly, both the anti-Russian and pro-Russian side of the current crisis are subcultures made up of a menagerie of such characters, as well as other more *organic* genetic material. Like any group, club, or organization the Russia support group is a societal melting pot imbued with myriad motivational norms. In these pages, I've already profiled grandmas and media executives, alongside political theorists and thrill seekers. If Vladimir Putin has a "troll army" such as western media antagonists suggest, then these soldiers joined up like patriots and mercenaries. As this book progresses, it should be crystal clear that no such troll army ever existed. Whatever motivated a couple of hundred ordinary people to influence the several million more, the fact that so few engaged so many with so much resource should have stunned the world. Somehow though, a real-life 300 Spartans epic has gone unnoticed by most.

Speaking of the troops of King Leonidas, I suppose the top Spartan actually had little to do with Spartan number three hundred. So, my own ignorance of people like special

Kremlin stooge Mark Chapman (mentioned by Bausman above) is normal. Chapman, who started blogging and commenting as the world's "Rambo of Russophiles" in July 2010, shares the same thread of indignation most of the rest of us do. He's been interviewed on some occasions, and each time reflects the same credible truth – utter distaste for Russophobia and lies. This quote from a Chapman talk with another "Kremlin Troll" named Anatoly Karlin, where the Kremlin Stooge relates experiences from Sochi similar to my own, it bears repeating here. Chapman, who initially engaged the anti-Russian throng at the infamous La Russophobe blog, talks with Karlin's audience about the deep hatred that fueled this current crisis:

> *"Prior to the initial accidental visit to La Russophobe, I was quite honestly unaware of that brand of barking mad Russophobia. I understood, of course, that bias against Russia existed, but there's some degree of bias against almost everybody, and I rationalized that some had good reasons to dislike Russia while others just thought they did. But there's a gulf of difference between reasoned disapproval and slobbering hate.[24]"*

Interestingly, it was Chapman who first debunked theories of

---

[24]   Interview with Mark Chapman (The Kremlin Stooge), Anatoly Karlin's blog, June 22, 2011.

Moscow paying hordes of troll agents in a post entitled *"Kremlin Troll Army Myth Deconstructed[25]"* for Russia Insider back in 2015. In the story, Chapman tells of the common practice across western mainstream media of censoring dissenting viewpoints. His references to Britain's Guardian deleting comments containing pertinent facts mirror what I've seen from my colleague Holger Eekhof at media such as Germany's ZEIT and others. Yes, Chapman, Eekhof, me or anybody else with a valid view is going to be provocative in a forum where the community is divided. And where the "message" is intended to follow a script, we often become the well intentioned and sometimes inadvertent provocateurs. In a way, it seems reasonable to say everybody is a troll or provocateur depending on the point of view.

Returning for a moment to Andrew Aaron Weisburd, the man who thinks himself the definitive expert on Putin's Internet agents, there were less than 400 Kremlin Trolls in May of 2015[26]. Weisburd's flawed metrics even went so far as to geolocate us Putin fanboys by country instead of reflecting reality. According to the Van Helsing in search of bloodless Kremlin agents, the clear majority of us reside in either the US, the Netherlands, Britain, Germany, Canada or Switzerland. This goes to show that witch hunters need not

---

25   "Kremlin Troll Army Myth Deconstructed", by Mark Chapman for Russia Insider, April 13, 2015.

26   "Geolocating Kremlin Trolls and Their Engaged Followers", by A. Aaron Weisburd, kremlintrolls.com, May 2015

be digital sociologists or analysts, but only religious zealots. I guess it never occurred to Weisburd to factor in arguments for and against Russia based on the countries with highest Internet proliferation? I'll just bet most NATO trolls come from the same countries using his methods. But this is all subjective for now.

The reason I bring Weisburd back in at this point is to make a point. For every one of the alleged 400 influential pro-Russian voices in social media, there are at least 100 anti-Russian "operatives." Just looking at the Twitter "follows" of Weisburd (@webradius) reveals a bizarre short-list of Putin haters. As an expert in social media myself, it's fair to ask the question, "Who in the hell follows the official Israel Defense Forces Twitter as their second act on that social network?" Israel, Israel, Israel, the Combating Terrorism Center at West Point, Khodorkovsky minion CNN's Michael Weiss, NATO, and General Philip Breedlove could serve to make up a lunatic Twitter psychoanalysis? Reading what Weisburd writes and what he tweets, the impartial observer would label him a psychotic stalker (or troll). He routinely tracked down noted pro-Russian journalists like RT's Mark Sleboda, calling him a traitor to the US because his view differs from the troll hunter's[27]. One thing I will say for this would be spy hunter, he's thorough when it comes to pointing fingers at those who disagree with Washington, London, Berlin, and Tel Aviv.

---

[27] "Raised Among Wolves, or Why Putin's Thugs Annoy Me", by A. Weisburd, kremlintrolls.com, February 2015

From Brazilian journalists Pepe Escobar to supposed "Putin man" *Baltnews* producer Alexander Kornilov, the ghosts and ghoul stories conjured to implicate all dissenting views remind me of the foolhardy anti-heroes from comic strips. If all these "subjects" are truly FSB operatives, the western world is doomed – not a shred of evidence supports Weisburd's or other Kremlin Ghostbuster's contentions.

Before I profile more Kremlin Trolls, it's important to mention that some real people are accused of being pawns of the former KGB operative named Putin. In this mixed up post-millennial world where ideology meets the Twilight Zone, ordinary citizens can and do become agents of change. Such is the case for another of Weisburd's "top trolls", Marilyn Justice (aka @mkj1951). So far, I've presented a Russia genius, several journalists, a publisher, an Amazon adventurer, and a grandma, so Marilyn's status as a retired Canadian stock trader turned Twitter warrior should certainly add flavor. Here's the story of the second of three top Kremlin Trolls from June 2015.

My Journey as a Top Kremlin Troll by Marilyn Justice

I got involved in all this when the 2014 Olympics were starting. You see, I am a classic stereotype of a Canadian, and of course, Hockey is my favorite game, with ice skating a close second. Since Russia is our classic rival on ice since the '72 Summit Series, it only made sense for me to be tuned to

Sochi.

So it was, I logged on to twitter and began looking for a reporter from one of the main countries to follow, but at the time I didn't know any Russian reporters or and RT or Sputnik announcers, so I followed the #Sochi hashtag for news. It was then I was stunned by the pure and open hatred of all things Sochi (and Russian) that was so apparent on Twitter and in mainstream media. It blew me away! Canada had just hosted the games in 2010, and we certainly had our problems with being ready on time, and the untimely death of the Georgian luger Nodar cast a shadow over our games too. Even with all the negative aspects of Vancouver though, we still weren't subjected to all the MSM journalist hatred.

Anyway, it was these same reporters that covered Vancouver tweeting about Ukraine, and the rioting in Kiev (the Maidan), so I was quite confused for some time because of the situation. I don't remember who I started following first in early days, maybe Marcel Sardo, Gleb Bazov, or perhaps Graham Phillips. I simply do not remember. I only know that figuring out "who was who" took a while and a lot of backtracking, watching videos, hashtags and so forth. I remember the Simon O / Vice videos and his feed - and reading twitter comments from people who didn't agree. Soon I figured out which twitter feeds agreed with what I was seeing, and then I began following those people. By the time of the referendum in Crimea, I was still stunned at the violence, while at the same time settled on who to trust for information.

Before the Crimea situation, I had found RT and Sputnik, Russia Insider, and a few others. Before these outlets came into my view, I only knew about how the US operated on a dim level, and it has been a steep learning curve for me to fully wake up. The journey has certainly eye opening, especially since I've never been to Europe or Russia. It is also interesting that anyone I know now on Twitter is through all of this. On the social and cultural level, I find Russians and Canadians are a lot alike, which is yet another awakening for me.

Returning to the media war and the injustice part, I recall most watching everything unfold, day by day, until the moment MH17 was brought down. At this point, I recalled a book I'd read by Norman Solomon about 8/9 years ago maybe - War Made Easy - how president's and pundits keep spinning us to death. This, added to the "message" being broadcast, clued me to the reality that the "real life" might become as messy and grotesque as Solomon's book.

I am not sure what else to tell Phil Butler's readers, only know that within one month I had figured out (in my mind, anyway) who the 'good guys' were and that they were not in Kiev or at the US State Department. I knew this because I watched their briefings every day for a long time and put out a "longtwit" of parts of the transcripts I thought were relevant. Then I switched to just reading the transcripts, instead of watching them lie, as it got too irritating.

At this point, I'm glad Phil Butler is telling our side. I remember when the New York Times writer asked me what I had to say about being named a top Kremlin troll, and how I have him Phil's name and information. As for the "list", I also told him that @webradius (Weisburd) was a basement dweller and a peeping Tom or stalker in my opinion. And that's my story, for what it is worth.

Marilyn Justice

For the reader Marilyn's recollection must hit a familiar chord when compared to my own or other trolls' histories. Her Kremlin escapades started with Sochi and unsportsmanlike conduct too. Putin and Russia were the targets, the western leadership might as well have lit up Sochi with laser sights for all to see. A proud nation welcomed the world to a true spectacle, and the new liberals and old warmongers ground their teeth and worked to spoil it, knowing the public would eat up the sarcasm, and nasty jibes, the stupid memes, and the spoiled brat American snowboarders – their gleaming shiny-white orthodontist smiles lighting up every major TV network. I remember pondering, "How could all that I was taught and all that I believed about sportsmanship be trampled like this?" As other Russian converts emerged from their cocoons, so did I. But for some, researchers and informers like The Saker, the conversion started much earlier.

My Dutch associate Holger Eekhof is not labeled in the elite tier of Putin fans like some others. The reason for this is simple and revealing. People passionate about politics and law are not listed among Putin's Praetorian troll guards for a good reason. Very few of the most notorious ones have political or philosophical backgrounds.

This fact brings us to the first revelation about the pro-Putin media army, the thing each has in common – their voice in media and social media. And the loudest voices for Russia outside RTTV and alternative news sources are – on Facebook and Twitter and on the social web. "We" (most of us) have social media in common, but there is another contingent out there – let's call them "the political purists." While you might include The Saker or even me in this category of geopolitical thinkers, the pure political animals argue differently. For one thing, people like Eekhof are more correctly labeled as "trolls" for their immutable sense at searching for argumentation.

I know that in Holger's case, his first endeavors to try and help change the rhetoric and thinking occurred in the comments sections of Germany's best "thinking journal" ZEIT. Yes, Eekhof is the quintessential comments troll, a man who would be Putin's highest paid troll, that is if the Russian president had the world's finest agitators on the payroll. On ZEIT, and later via Sputnik Germany, Eekhof smashed like bugs scores of so-called NATO trolls with his researcher doggedness.

It's important for people to understand not just social media, but the two-way conversation that exists underneath 140 characters and a Facebook cat share, the space underneath the messages in those comments sections. Eekhof, while adding to the dialogue about Russia at ZEIT, had no fewer than 14 successive identities. This was due to his handle "The Frenchman" being banned outright each time the argument grew heated. The "passion" for politics in arguments about ideals is strong beneath social media. Holger took some time away from Sputnik the other day to tell us how and why he came to the aid of mother Russia in German social media venues. Here is his brief Kremlin Troll autobiography, translated from the German.

How I Became a Putin Troll by Holger Eekhof

First, let me be clear. I am not a Putin Troll. I am a Europa Troll.

Now, as to how I got here...

Politics has always been my hobby. I studied political science back in the 1990's under noted Professor Hans W. Maull, a member of the Trilateral Commission at the University of Trier. Later on, I became active in the Christian Democratic (CDU) party, which certainly did not predestine me to become a pro-Russian activist. As a loyal CDU operative, I was expected to be firmly anchored in the "Western" camp.

Unfortunately, this so-called "Western camp" and those iconic "Western values" are no longer existent here in the West. Those "values," if they ever existed, have drastically eroded since the fall of the Soviet Union. Today, the mere mention of them is an absurdity, for they are simply no longer existent, no longer present.

The most obvious example of this "absurdity" is a rumor Europeans cling to in a fabulously fond way – liberty being above all tenets the beacon our Lord alias partner the USA beckons us with. As we see, the faux democracy has led American and thus all of Europe into bondage - and thereby a masquerade of freedom. And so, this reality became so perverse for me, that I could no longer be silent as a learned representative of Western values. From my personal doorstep, the following event helped chart my new course.

Georgia's attack on South Ossetia, as a matter of coincidence, manifested in a clear (to me) revelation that Georgia bore the sole blame for the war. This was also clear to every citizen in Tbilisi. And even to any member of the ENM. But how then could such a distortion of reality come through our media? This was and is the question that guides me. I am about solutions, and here is the only one I see.

Those who have gathered around Saakashvili and who have benefited from corruption through their anti-corruption system, they have bought their impunity to the "West" by making an absolutely senseless war. This war was a deliberate and intentional lie from the start, and not only through the so-called Mainstream Media. For the perpetrators, all of them, Russia was evil, and the facts did not matter anymore.

The Georgian people and their historical ties with Russia became the game of geopolitical arrogance. Georgian soldiers were sacrificed to maintain the legitimacy of NATO. A legitimation which has been more than questioned by Russia's approach to Europe. The United States' rule instrument was simply the source of erosion, and a Saakashvili was sold enough to send his soldiers to death for demonstration purposes-in the service of the master.

At this point, I almost turned the page. From a transatlantic and a globalist to a European.

Holger Eekhof

Chapter IX: Actors in the Epopee

*"People are always teaching us democracy but
the people who teach us democracy don't want
to learn it themselves."*
Vladimir Putin

If the civil war afire in the East of Ukraine had happened a
thousand years ago the children of the Kievan Rus' would
have gathered around a campfire to sing the Byliny[28] or
Stariny about the heroes saving them from an uncertain fate.
Those forms of epic poems from the 9th century AD took on
all too familiar themes I've witnessed via my friends and
colleagues in the Donbass. The crisis exacted on the people
of Ukraine by outside forces really should be required
through an oral history, the injustice and the heroic energy
buried in Novorossiya. In my mind's eye, there is planted
themes that Byliny singers might have sung. A mother
bidding a son farewell, a fighter saddling his horse or
departing over the wall of some great medieval city, the epic
journey begun and even exchanging taunts with an enemy
appears in my consciousness – blood brothers and living and
dead heroes. For those unfamiliar with the structure of these

---

[28] Bylina, plural byliny, traditional form of Old Russian and Russian heroic
narrative poetry transmitted orally. Encyclopedia Britannica online.

Slavic poems, 'older' heroes in the songs resembled mythological figures, while the younger heroes more closely resembled normal human beings. As the fates would have it, there are modern bogatyr[29] in this story too. The first person who comes to mind when I think of the heroes of the Donbass, Russell "Texas" Bonner Bentley is an American writer and volunteer soldier who traveled on his own from Texas to serve in the Novorossiyan Armed Forces (NAF). While Russell may not resemble either of the three most famous bogatyrs, Dobrynya Nikitich, Ilya Muromets, and Alyosha Popovich, the adventurous side of Bentley, Graham Phillips, and people like photojournalists Patrick Lancaster do remind me of other ancient heroes. Talking with these friends for background for this book, "Texas" mentioning Baldr, the Norse hero who is most famous for his demise, rather than his earthly deeds. It is right here the roles foreign agents played in the Donbass fight takes on a rather epic tone. While Bentley, Phillips, and others may not fit the classic "hero" frame West of Donetsk, I know the people there do hold them up as icons. In this way, they occupy locally the same pedestals Motorola and Givi did, and will surely be found worthy of their own Byliny. I find it ironic that "Texas" would mention his the "son of Thor" as a childhood hero. So many people in the Donbass acquaint

---

[29] Bogatyr (Russian: богатырь) a stock character or knight-errant in medieval East Slavic legends, Russiapedia from RT, *Written by Oleg Dmitriev*

him and these others with "good," as is the case of Baldr. And it's rather epic to me too, that the death of Baldr was sung as the harbinger of Ragnarök, an apocalyptic moment where the fates converge into a kind of *"Twilight of the Gods."* Many of us prophesied that the Ukraine Civil War would lead to some mutually shared destruction of our world shuld Putin not prevail on reason somehow.

While it's true the exploits of these westerners are not so well-known outside Ukraine and Russia, it's also clear that in Ukraine they represent a kind of omen. Bentley, Phillips, commanders Motorola and Givi, and unsung heroes like their slain comrade Ruslan Shchedrov, callsign "Filin (owl) are characters in a would be a Greek tragedy. As I watched the special Phillips did of Filin's wedding, and then learned a sniper's bullet took his life recently, a hundred more such sad stories flooded my mind. How many mourn with the families these brave people? While certainly there are morning families on both sides of this conflict, the pointed lack of coverage of this war by BBC and others guaranteed a coalition of dissent would form. It is from these instances of injustice and untruth that Putin's "Kremlin Troll" forces were empowered to take on a multi-trillion-dollar media empire. The focused negative attention onto Donetsk and toward the Russian side of this crisis, helped produce and different and even more powerful emotional response. Creating martyrs and then disrespecting them is just idiotic PR in my book. It is this dumb strategy and mindset the anti-Russia cabal clings to somehow. The notion anything can silence the cries of outrage and pain of victims for long. This brings me to the real epic heroes in every conflict of the human spirit, the unsung fighters Reuters or TIME can never seem to find.

One of Putin's most powerful soldiers is a relatively unsung Kremlin hero named Jeffrey Silverman, a former US Army weapons specialist who became a sort of castaway in the Republic of Georgia. Our paths first began to intertwine after I had left Russia Inside and when I began writing editorial and research for New Eastern Outlook in July 2015. Since that time, I have had more social media communications with Silverman, than with any other single "agent" of pro-Russian support. This is due in large part to Silverman's unmatched ability to transform thought and research into useful information. His story, like that of my Amazon troll buddy Eric Anderson, is wrought with fascinating details, adventure, and even dangerous exchanges with the world of spy spooks, etc. I'll give my further assessment on Silverman farther along, but who better to frame his contribution to the Putin plan than the man who always says he "rides-with-the-fox-and-runs-with-the-hounds!"

Jeff Silverman - Too Educated for His Own Good

I, Jeffrey K. Silverman, have been blamed for many things, not only being a Kremlin hack, AKA, troll, but an American agent, NOK, non-official contact, and most recently a CIA agent who penetrated one of the alternative news sites closest to the Kremlin, New Eastern Outlook, NEO, under the auspices of the Russian Academy of Science, Institute for Oriental Studies. I am also the Bureau Chief for Veterans Today, which has its following, a sordid bunch.

We have something in common; we took our oaths on the US Constitution Dead Serious – to defend the US from all enemies foreign and domestic. If that means using any media outlet outside of the MSM to get our word across, so be it and good riddance to anyone who takes exception.

But it all started back at Fort Knox Kentucky, Home of Armor, when I was trained as a Forward Observer - or Calvary Scout, dating back to 1981. The cold war was still hot, and we were told that our life expectancy was short when the shit hit the fan.

Fortunately, it did not during the Carter years. However, that MOS only was useful later in life when I started working for an international tobacco company. I was growing and buying tobacco in Brazil, China, Georgia, Azerbaijan and Central Asia. Later when the British Company that I worked for got bought out by an American one, I have booted out the door, three months' severance and ended up back in the US at the ripe age of 42. I decided to finally finish my MSc degree. Then I headed back to Georgia,

To make a long story short, I ended up at the Patterson School of Diplomacy, University of Kentucky—one of the so called "spy-finishing schools" in the US at a Land Grant Institution. I got my MSc plus in vocational agriculture and could take all the Patterson coursework to my heart's content, diplomacy, and international law.

Anyway, I ended up with too much education for my own good and too much experience; I could see too many things – make too many connections and when working for a US-funded NGO, United Methodists Committee for Relief, UMCOR, as an agricultural program director, I was naïve to report suspected corruption to the home office and got my "at will" contact cancelled the last day, and they tried to put me on the next flight back to the US.

I stayed, investigated, took a job as a copy editor for the Georgian Times, and the Embassy had me fired from that too. Soon I connected the pieces together and learned that the US State Department was using a US Department of Agriculture "Food for Peace Program" to fund Chechen fighters, your freedom fighter is my terrorist.

I learned all the details and opened the story in Georgia, and then the problems started. The murder of Roddy Scott, based on information provided by the OCSE sealed my fate; I was picked up on the order of the US Embassy and beaten in Azerbaijan the next day. And then my passport was later revoked by the US government and declared a non-national of the US, left without any passport in Azerbaijan. Having an old Georgian one, Joni Simonishvili, proved useful in jumping the border back to Georgia and out of the hands of the US Embassy and their Azeri enforcers.

As I wrote Roddy Scott, a British Journalist, about the notes that I had compiled when investigating corruption in the US funded NGOs ... "share it with those who really want to get to the bottom of what is happening in Georgia and Pankisi."

It was soon clear that US and Georgian Special Services admitted outright that they were working together with the Chechens, blowing somebody up in a toilet (perhaps it was Vepkhia Margoshvili). That is where my life changed. I am, was just a guy who found himself down and out, low on cash and wrote some articles to pay the bills.

It was clear when we compared notes, which was fascinating and certainly started filling in a few blanks for me. Here are a few things I have heard from the Chechens themselves. All this comes from guys I know in Pankisi.

1. Georgian generals, who have actually come to his house in Duisi, have regularly visited Khamzat Gelayev.

2. Georgian soldiers regularly sell weapons to the Chechen muj in Pankisi.

3. Last year's foray into Abkhazia was entirely organized by the Georgians, and they even sent a number of their own special forces with the Chechens. These Special Forces are the same people who man the checkpoints to Pankisi.

4. The Georgians are interested in clamping down on

Arabs in Pankisi, but not Chechens. Apparently, three prominent Arabs were snatched at the checkpoint on the bridge a while back.

The kidnapping was very much a JV between Georgians and Chechens. And, yes, they had to pay twice. The guy who held them captive is called Imran Akhmadov, a person that I know quite well. He is the brother of Ramazan Akhmadov, who was killed Jan 2001.

As I saw myself, sneaking in and out of Pankisi several times, "there were plenty of boyeviks [Chechen fighter] in Pankisi, and pretty much they operate openly; but the story has never really come out because most journals don't have access."

And there is a real danger of kidnapping if you are there too long without the protection of a Chechen commander. Equally, the Chechens have a vested interest in making sure the full story never comes out (in print, photos or TV). It's the kind of thing that might just provoke the Russians to do something, (or give them an excuse, I guess).

As Roddy Scott, who was killed in 2002, wrote me just before his death.

> *"As you mention all too clearly, there is a very cozy relationship there between the Chechens and the Georgians. Hence most journals have got the right end of the stick, but have never had the sources to back it up.*

On the Arab side of things, I confess I'm a bit hazy. But the guys have told me there are plenty of Arabs there, some of whom have married locally. (I have only ever met a couple of Arabs, and that was a 2000 trip across the mountains to Chechnya with 30 other Chechen fighters). But I have my doubts about the 'Al Qaeda recent arrivals.' From what you say it seems that it might all be an excuse to increase US toe hold in the region.

Again, would be very interested in comparing notes with you. Seems that there is a lot we might be able to piece together if we sit down and swap info. Oh yes, re Azerbaijan. First time I went to Baku, (en route to Pankisi in 2000), I stayed in flat with half a dozen wounded guys who had been treated in Baku. A year later, back in Pankisi, I bumped into some of them again, recovered and ready to get back into action."

Fast Forward

Having been here since 1991, in Georgia, has been a front row seat for a region which has been thrown back into a rerun of the Great Game. All the while the Russians are trying to retain their influence, while the Americans and British are strengthening their foothold in the region. With the attention of such powerful forces, regional leaders have begun to exercise their positions. The Chechens and Georgians have formed a secret strategic alliance against the

Russians, Azerbaijan turns a blind eye and allows financial support and medical aid, and now the Georgians are attempting to reunify their country by quashing the small semi-autonomous Russian-oriented regions in the country, namely the breakaway Georgian regions of South Ossetia and Abkhazia.

Ukraine has become part of this game too, and having known one of the snipers sent there to help start the revolution has prevented me from trying to cross any borders. It took 15 years to get back my revolved passport, and happenstance, on the day that Trump was elected. One thing is clear, and the focus of my articles and interviews in the international, Georgian and Russian media, much money has been wasted in bolstering Georgia's military, to fight "international terrorism" but this too may have been part of the New Great Game, and it is but a pretext for Georgia to put teeth into what they wanted to be gunboat diplomacy in regaining territorial integrity; and the lion share of what I have witnessed is linked to much US foreign policy, especially in terms of the T & E program which was primarily directed towards preparing to attack Abkhazia (as opposed to fighting terrorist in the Pankisi Valley).

The Georgian argument stems from their contention that separatist regimes breed terrorism and this should be addressed through the T&E and other assistance programs. Regardless, instability in Pankisi has been a primary source of tension between Russia and Georgia. American military advisors arrived in Georgia in April 2002, allegedly, "on a mission to contain al Qaeda loyalists" who may be operating there.

Instead of terrorist using the instability to their ends, it may be the United States that is guilty of exploiting the chronic instability in Georgia for larger geopolitical games and that now extends to Syria, Iran, Ukraine, and this is where my attention has been in recent years, chasing weapons, the transit of Chechen fighters and other sorts of terrorists.

My further work in Georgia include diving into what was going on with weapons programs, digging into how the US under Bush Junior encouraged Georgia to start the war over South Ossetia as part of the U.S. Election President Campaign back in 2008, the appearance of bio weapons labs in Georgia, the footprint of Bechtel National in pseudo-civilian peaceful projects, and Georgia becoming a transit "conduit" country for weapons and foreign fighters, not to mention a hub for drug smuggling and arms for weapons swaps.

And in recent years, tracking these networks and friends and foes, and the links with Turkey and Syria, it has been clear that most Chechen commanders have shelf lives, not necessarily regarding effectiveness on the battlefield but in terms of political usefulness. It seems that another one is about to find out the hard way that Chechens are only there to further objectives they don't hold themselves, not become glorious martyrs able to pass unimaginable wealth on to their families.

As I have documented in many of my articles, Chechens were supported via an NGO funded by USAID and the U.S. State Department, which used these funds, not for humanitarian purposes but to support aggressive and covert operations.

The presence of Chechens in Georgia was used to justify the 64 million-dollar U.S. Train and Equip Program, purportedly established to fight international terrorism, which was a means of using Georgia to gain a greater toe hold in the region and use it as a regional forward operating base for future wars. Georgian military bases, port facilities and air bases have been upgraded with the objective of being eventually employed by U.S., Israeli and NATO troops."

My greatest claim to fame and causing the US Embassy to put on their website that I cannot be considered a reliable source of information is the story that I broke about the bio weapons programs in Georgia.

The US Embassy to Georgia has released a statement about Mikheil Saakashvili's former American advisor Jeffrey Silverman's interview published in the 'Kvela Siakhle' newspaper. 'The United States strongly supports freedom of speech and the press and has long advocated for a free and pluralistic media environment in Georgia and elsewhere. Nevertheless, with editorial freedom comes responsibility, including the responsibility to corroborate information before reporting it. The interview excerpts Kviris Palitra published today on its website, and Facebook page, contains some statements about U.S. policy that are without any basis in fact, and that, unfortunately, reflect on the veracity of their obvious source', the report says. Silverman talks about several topics in the interview, including PM Zurab Zvhania's death.

Even more scandals than that, UN took me serious over the false flag over the Khurcha Incident, 2008, and the Russians and many in the International Community over the bio weapons labs in Georgia and Ukraine. Even the VOA came out against my word as part of the damage control to the documentary that I helped – supplying detailed design plans for the lab and reports of deaths associated with bio weapons and gas. This knowledge put me in a good position, as even the alleged Sarin attack, crossing the red line in Syria proved an America scripted false flag. It is a real recommendation for a Kremlin Troll when VOA is on the attack.

There is lots of history in this "love-hate" relationship with my so-called American Embassy, especially since I have American Indian roots on my mother's side, and we escaped the trail of tears in 1838. American Citizen Services is no friend.

Anyway, I hope this summary will help you better understand how I am supposedly working on the other side, done been flipped ... but where are the money and passport?

I like what others write about me, under one of my other names, "Joni Simonishvili' was/is the pen-name of Jeffrey K. Silverman, and this is not the only revelation to come from the pen of this investigative journalist as Abkhaz World.

For example, one article back in begins with an explanation of how this observer was able to recognize at a glance the reason for the construction of the concrete ramp in Mingrelia, West Georgia and how this was a tank unloading platform.

At the time, I was working for Georgian State TV (1st Channel) as well as the Human Rights' Center in Tbilisi, though (for the sake of my job) I did not want to advertise that I was checking into such things. I completed my training as a 19D Forward Observer (Scout) at Fort Knox (Kentucky, USA) in my youth (1981). This is the US home of Armour (Armour School) — and I was trained in recon and armour (tanks and tracks, APCs).

My training was to enable me to destroy Soviet Armor, call for fire, and basically go behind front lines, "first in and last out." There was no doubt in my mind as to what the Georgians had constructed with this loading platform "tank station" and the reason for its existence so close to the border with the [Georgian region] of Abkhazia.

I continue to write under this name. In 2004, I was issued with a document stating that I am not a national of the US, and this is most likely related to my investigation into the situation in the Pankisi Valley [north-eastern Georgia], specifically as to how money was being supplied to Chechens from a US government NGO in close cooperation with Georgian Security Agencies, and how, in addition, this was a carefully crafted ploy both to justify the 64 million dollar US Train and Equip Program and to gain a larger toehold in the region. The funding mechanism behind the cozy relationship between the US and Georgian governments was something I investigated with British journalist Roddy Scott, who was killed during the investigation. I even went on Russian TV (Russian State TV Company-VESTI) and spilled the beans on this Pankisi operation.

I also invested the murder and cover up of the Georgian Prime Minister and got the investigation reopened and described in detail how the FBI destroyed forensic evidence. All that is well documented on the internet, as well as various US and European mechanism about gun running, and links to the US and gun running John McCain.

Over the years, I have also looked into events (dating from 2003) in South Ossetia, Abkhazia, and Adjaria (on behalf of International Crisis Group, between 2002 and 2004, and other clients, including some Western European countries, NATO members to boot).

I have information on how there were several Americans, Cubic Corporation, and other US contractors, who helped organize some of the dirty tricks in the Gal District, West

Georgia; how they were also involved in training the Georgian snipers let loose in July and August 2008 in the South Ossetian zone of conflict.

The same snipers were later used in Ukraine as part of the effort of the US to pull Ukraine fully into the sphere of the West. These same trainers ("snipers") were bragging about how South Ossetia was going to be a cake walk. A US organized sniping campaign started before the attack on South Ossetia, killing civilians, which is a war crime (as I was taught in my days as a 19D in the US army).

I had the date of the war THREE months before the actual attack on South Ossetia (August 2008) from USG defense contractors, who thought that I was one of theirs, as I talk the military B[ull] S[hit] got them drunk, and they started spilling the beans.

The fact of my knowledge about the approximate date of the attack can be confirmed by the Human Rights' Center in Tbilisi, as I shared my experience with them about two months before the actual Georgian attack on South Ossetia (7 August). On about 2 August 2008, Georgian police went into border-villages and confiscated small arms from locals. They knew the war was coming but decided not to pull back civilians out of harm's way, which was an intentional act, worse than malfeasance.

I went on record about my knowledge of the US government's possible involvement in war crimes, its alleged role in weapons' trafficking, and even earlier (in 2005), when there were armed skirmishes in South Ossetia, and officials from the US Defense Department were involved in direct support for an engagement with South Ossetian forces.

I can provide more by way of a truthful history of the events of August 2008. As a veteran of the US Army, I have also been investigating weapons' trafficking; I have been on Georgian TV (Maestro Channel), where I shared my insights and various documents.

I blew open a story on weapons' trafficking several months ago involving flights out of Georgia. I worked two years for Georgian State TV (1st Channel). I was behind Russian lines in August 2008 in South Ossetia, investigating human rights' violations and got into an ammo-dump full of Serbian weapons, which reached Georgia via Jordan. I have copies of the end-user certificate and have investigated, together with Georgian TV, many of these networks.

I also discovered where Israeli cluster-bombs fell on Georgian villages, even before Human Rights' Watch came out with their report, and these cluster-bombs even killed some Georgian soldiers.

Quiet American

I have always contended that the rights and wrongs of the disputes are not my main concern, but everyone should unite against the use of cluster-bombs, against the staging of incidents such as occurred in the Mingrelian village of Khurcha, where a bus carrying citizens from Abkhazia's Gal District to vote in Georgia's parliamentary elections (May 2008) was subjected to Georgian gunfire just after it had crossed into Mingrelia so that the attack could be falsely attributed to the Abkhazians, and against the carrying out of politically motivated wars by a state against its own citizens. Having spent some nights behind Russian lines, both in South Ossetia and the buffer-zone, I visited an abandoned Georgian weapons' stockpile in the South Ossetian zone of conflict; it had been left unguarded when the Georgian army fled in panic. This was the event that helped me put together the final pieces, based on pulling labels and the weapons left behind, of how Georgia is used to transit weapons for the US government – and Georgia is not the end user.

Georgia has long been recognized as a transit-point for illegal trade in weapons and terrorists, and much has been organized under the banner of the US government and funded by USAID (United States Agency for International Development), and even the US Department of Agriculture and US State Department.

It is now clear to me that there has been a "big connection" between the cluster-bomb makers and many high officials in the Georgian government and in the MOD. BTW, my articles and documents provided the US Embassy just before getting my passport back, may have been considered a form of blackmail. It worked, and in any event, the Russians know what no good the Americans and their NATO partners are up to, poor Georgia!

Jeff Silverman

As the reader has no doubt gleaned, Silverman is a wealth of information on the wild and crazy goings on in the Caucasus. A brave guy, or one some would call "crazy" for his blatant stance in front of "less than savory" characters there in Tbilisi, Jeff's a sort of legend in the clandestine community of journalists. I'll never forget a conversation concerning him I once had with Veterans Today Managing Editor Jim Dean a few years back. We were talking about the CIA's role in Georgia and other former Soviet states when the subject of Silverman even still being alive came up. Dean, who's known Jeff longer than I, said he was amazed "they" had not already gotten to him. Given the size of thorn Silverman has been in the side of spooks and sellout politicians operating inside the Caucasus, it's not hard to understand what the VT editor meant. And while almost all of us pro-Russia activists have suffered some degree of pain over our vehemence, Silverman has been beaten and worse for his efforts.

The many war reporters, freedom fighters, independent investigators, and local activists and insurgents have been part of the heroic prose of this insane new kind of information war. But there is another kind of heroic figure most people fail to recognize. Influential as any photojournalist, crazy as any moral insurrectionist, the social-media warlords for Putin operate in a sort of "make believe" digital realm akin to online political war gaming. While the term "troll" has been applied to so many of us media "operators," Russia's most important envoys often operate more like social superheroes, who appear ready to thwart any enemy onslaught by the sheer might of willpower or numbers. One such digital dynamo is a Cambridge research fellow, Dr. Chris Doyle, whom I first met on Facebook three years ago. Doyle, who help build several of the largest Russian support communities on Facebook, has undergone a different kind of "punishment" and ordeal in the name of free speech. Once again, rather than attempting to explain in my own words this Kremlin agent's path, the Facebook super-sleuth is best characterized in his own words.

Chris Doyle: Kremlin Facebook Agent

My fascination with Russia began in 1976 when, as a 10-year-old boy, I was mesmerized by the performances of the Soviet gymnast, Nikolai Andrianov, at the Montreal Olympics. He won 5 Gold Medals and was far-and-away the most successful athlete at the games. At the same time, I fell in love with the Soviet National Anthem. In those days, the UK won very little, and so the BBC was compelled to broadcast the medal ceremonies of overseas gold medal winners. Of all the national hymns, I found that of the USSR especially powerful and emotive.

Shortly afterward, I bought an LP of Russian music ("Russian Fireworks"). I still remember the playlist (Kamennoi Ostrov, Procession of the Sardar, Sabre Dance, The Song of the Volga Boatmen, Polyushka Polye (Meadowland) and the Finale of Tchaikovsky's 1812 Overture. My love of Russian culture was crystallized. I still have the sleeve although the record was lost long ago when my parents moved back to Ireland.

I started to support the USSR in all sports but especially in gymnastics, athletics, football, ice-skating and ice-hockey. Throughout the 1980's, I followed Soviet sports-stars like Nikolai Andrianov, Yelena Davydova, Svetlana Boginskaya, Vladislav Tretiak, Valeriy Kharlamov, Irina Rodnina, Yuriy Seydik, Natalia Lisovskaya, Olga Bryzgina and Vasiliy Alekseyev with passion.

These events inspired a life-long love for the Soviet Union and Russia and, as a boy, I was always delighted to read that USSR had more nuclear weapons, more tanks, and more soldiers than NATO. I also used to enjoy watching the Victory Day parade from Moscow's Red Square on the BBC, and I was a huge fan of Leonid Brezhnev.

Following the collapse of the USSR in 1991 (due to 45 years

of economic and political interference from the US, UK and other members of the Common Market), I became a fierce opponent of western intervention in other nations, and I began to detest NATO. This hatred was fueled by being Irish by birthright; I've always abhorred the UK and British imperialism.

My sadness at the collapse of the Soviet Union was made worse by having to watch Boris Yeltsin make a drunken fool of himself on the BBC news. Throughout the Yeltsin years, my interest in Russia waned. However, the rise of Russia under Vladimir Putin saw my love of Russia return with a vengeance. It also coincided with my divorce in November 1999. From 1999 to present, all of my girlfriends and partners have been born in the USSR. This was due to the appalling behavior of my English ex-partner regarding our son. I've always known Russian girls have superior family values.

My love of the USSR and Russia has been greatest for the last 7 years (after meeting a girl from the Donbass; Russian mother; Ukrainian father; in 2010). Although this relationship ended in 2012, it has given me a special love and respect for the people in this region. I've spent a considerable time within the historical borders of "Novorossiya" (as far west as Zaporizhia), and I find these people the warmest I've ever met anywhere on earth. They remind me of the country-folk I met in Ireland as a child. Like anyone who loves Russia, I was dismayed and angered by the violent riots and shootings that took place in Ukraine in February 2014 ('Euromaidan') and which culminated in the ousting of the democratically-elected President, Viktor Yanukovych.

Like many people on Facebook, this was when I joined several pro-Russian groups (including "INTERNATIONAL FRIENDS OF RUSSIA," which had 40,000 members). I also set up my own group "Friends and Lovers of Russia" (which reached 205,000 members). Sadly, BOTH groups were hacked and neutralized in February 2017 (I believe with approval and assistance from Facebook employees). Euromaidan has seen a sea change in Ukraine's sociopolitical system – including shifts towards the EU, USA and even fascism. The US (of course) is now calling the shots in Kiev (and has been since Victoria Nuland and Geoffrey Pyatt, were heard discussing their plans to mold Ukraine according to US interests in 2014).

Thankfully, there were – simultaneously – numerous pro-Russian demonstrations in Eastern and Southern Ukraine and, shortly afterward, Vladimir Putin intervened in the Crimea and sent a Russian military intervention to protect the majority Russian population there. A referendum took place in which over 90% of Crimean residents voted to leave Ukraine and rejoin Russia. In the Donbass, the Donetsk and Lugansk oblasts also held referenda and voted overwhelmingly to leave Ukraine and become independent states. Unfortunately, without the protection of the Russian Armed forces, these regions have been targeted for retribution by the Ukrainian Army, and tens of thousands of innocent civilians have been indiscriminately killed. Since the US-EU funded Euromaidan in February 2014, I have been politically active in social media supporting Russia, Vladimir Putin, Crimean reunification with Russia and the Donbass (Novorossiya). I have also been a vocal opponent of the US, UK, EU and NATO (and their roles in provoking war in Ukraine and elsewhere). In addition, I have changed my lifestyle to support Russia and the Donbass financially whenever possible.

I buy all of my gifts and luxury items from Russia, I support Russian charities, I financially support Russian media and I financially help selected people who have been injured by the bombs of the Ukrainian Army. Realistically, all of my disposable income goes to Russia, and this equates to several thousand pounds a year. Also, I have refused to travel to the UK and the EU since February 2014. I intend to continue this pro-Russian (anti-western) lifestyle for life (or until the EU removes sanctions against Russia and adopts a MUCH friendlier approach towards Moscow). Moreover, I have changed my Last Will and Testament to leave my home, all of its contents and all of my savings (currently £218,000) to a Russian Charity.

Chris Doyle

A big fan of Russia, quite obviously, Doyle's recollection above betrays my "common thread" assertions even still. Russian expats, spouses of Russians, history buffs fascinated with the world's biggest country or dedicated Russophiles the organic and the inorganic Kremlin trolls share an appalling root motivation for their outcries – the indiscriminate killing in the Donbass and elsewhere over "old world" imperialism. Doyle, just like me or any other American "convert," just went all-in over the injustice. For my part, I have insulated a bit from Facebook or Twitter retribution by my "first adopter" and status in the tech community from days gone by. As for Doyle and others like him, getting banned from any social network is a simple matter of the network acting on a single complaint. While I may be banned tomorrow, the ramifications for any network are different depending on many factors. Whatever the reasons or strategies employed by social media, Doyle and many others have suffered a lot of friction over the years. While it's fair to say these Kremlin agents did their fair share of administering some pain on NATO and globalists trolls too, I've yet to see a Russophobe or State Department hack banned from a social network. Bombastic as Chris Doyle might be, the fake news and propaganda he fights against are far more onerous in the end. I like the man, just to be totally honest, and I know he's been called "traitor" and a lot worse, just like the rest of us. If this new brand of warfare we are witnessing is ever made into an epic poem, it's for certain many of the people I mention herein will be named. At the extreme, battlefield casualties like Russia One cameraman *Anatoly Klyan, who was shot in the stomach* as the bus he was riding in came under fire by Ukrainian forces, *or reporter* Igor Kornelyuk and his cameraman Anton Voloshin, who had mortar fire called down upon them by the *Ukrops*[30], create the real martyrs of freedom of speech and the press.

What we are witnessing is a totally new kind of geo-political crisis or war. The new west-east crisis my Kremlin Troll friends are taking part in is an asymmetrical war with a never before seen harmonized social, media, and even military component. What I mean by this is, embedded journalists are now joined by ordinary citizens both on the battlefield and off, all relaying information outward from points of the crisis. The speed of communication is what differentiates this new world crisis from the past Cold War, for instance. Perhaps the most important facet of this new communications warfare paradigm is the way the public can become inextricably tied to the war correspondent or even the combatants themselves. A fine example of this is how another unsung Kremlin hero named James Beagan, who goes by the handle C.I.D.P. Astronaut (@The_Jag_10). When Donbass militia leader Motorola and Givi were cut down by

---

[30] In the war-torn Donetsk and Luhansk Oblasts the term Ukrops indicates Ukrainian soldiers and volunteer fighters – Kiev Post, *Ukrainian wartime glossary: Ukrop, Vatnik and more* – January of 2015

assassins in Donetsk, James' connectivity to the war and its heroes showed the strange connectivity I mention here. From battles and exploits on the battlefield, to the geopolitical gameplay in the world parliaments the pro-Russia band never had to really "troll" at all. Just waking up provided all needed impetus for fighting the flawed narrative. Right here is the appropriate time to introduce you to a truth seeker, a comrade who's never failed the message.

C.O.D.P Astronaut: People, Propaganda & Putin

My name is James Beagan, aged 53 and a working-class guy from Glasgow but now living on the Island of Gigha on the West Coast of Scotland's Inner Hebrides.

I've worked in various sectors, including education until

becoming ill 5 years ago with C.I.P.D. Even though this ailment has prevented me from working as I once did, (classed as disabled), I can still think, and I can still have a voice.

Since an early age, I was fascinated by history and politics and I quickly realized that both have an impact on all aspects of our lives. Since I grew up during the Cold War, I later came to realize that what was being reported by western media (MSM) and especially here in the UK, was biased against, our allies during The Great Patriotic War. Russia's role in just about everything amounted to propaganda & lies from both media and politicians here on a daily basis.

Then came the Fall of the Berlin Wall and the end of USSR and the Warsaw Pact, Yeltsin, the Berlin Understanding/ Agreement and through the democratic election process Vladimir Putin.

At this point the EU, the US (NATO) had the opportunity to welcome the new Russian Federation as an equal partner that would benefit all country's. The potential for further nuclear disarmament, peace, economic trading benefits was at hand. But this did start to happen. Instead, vested interests within the US and the vassal State that is the UK stopped this great potential for humanity.

The US and the EU under the guise of NATO broke the Berlin agreement and perused a policy of encirclement and a policy of trying to destabilize Russia politically and economically.

These policies brought about the rise of western backed Islamist-extremism in Afghanistan then Chechnya, terror attacks in Russia, NGO's backing groups against President Putin democratically elected Govt & ultimately the western run coup of Ukraine.

Watching this unfolding here in the UK, I was horrified to see and hear politicians, privately owned MSM and the state-run BBC churn out lie after lie - day after day – to a waiting UK society.

I decided to try to do something about this misinformation and propaganda, and chose the medium of Twitter.

To tell the truth from my own eyes of what I knew, and to comment on world events, this seemed an apt mission for me. I also decided to say the truth about Vladimir Putin and highlight what he said in his speeches and in his actions, and to show the facts that he sought partnership (on equal terms) with the countries of the world.

In observing and sharing these few years, I consider V. Putin to be the best politician that the World has seen in decades. The Russian leader promotes economic trading partnerships, societal understanding, fighting terrorism and its causes in commonality, scientific partnership, stability, equal rights, diplomacy and most importantly the idea that all countries should adhere to international law.

Putin is one of the few Leaders who, when giving a speech or interview, is unafraid to speak the Truth on issues. This openness is one reason why he is so popular around the world.

The people of the west are awakening to the state intel MSM lies regarding Russia, and V. Putin. Attitudes are changing but after so many years of brainwashing there are still many who believe the lies but with voices like my own are trying to make an impact and inroads into opposing and overturning the lies.

It's a fight that will continue, and one I believe we must and will win.

Political change is coming to the UK, the paradigm of EU - US relations will change, and I hope with that change then we can work in partnership with Russia. To that end I became supporter or "Kremlin troll" as Putin's detractors would say.

"Everyone has a voice, everyone no matter what age or class, so use yours to make change and to unite people."
C.I.D.P Astronaut – Master Kremlin Troll

James Beagan

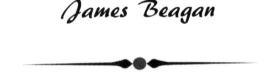

Amazingly, my many Tweets, shares, and conversations with James never touched on his devastating illness. Like so many who suffer from such afflictions, he minimizes his own suffering while at the same time helping others in what small ways he can. I only woke up to the realization of what C.I.D.P. stands for on reading the biography he sent me. Such is the nature of the 140-character limit on Twitter, and of our social interactions overall. To be so acutely aware of facts and data about Syria (for instance), and to be obtuse to the human reality sitting at the other end of a DSL connection is an endemic digital reality. It's interesting to ponder whether those "NATO Trolls," who accuse us all, ever take a fragment of a moment to discover who we really are? As I delve further into my Kremlin agent colleagues, I am more and more sure they do not.

Chapter X: Putin's Proxy War Praetorians

"Thirteen years after the end of the Soviet Union, the American press establishment seemed eager to turn Ukraine's protested presidential election on November 21 into a new cold war with Russia."

Stephen F. Cohen

By late 2015 the complexion of the West-East crisis had blossomed into an unparalleled confrontation where old and new geo-strategies metamorphosed into sheer chaos. The results of the so called "Arab Spring" across North Africa and parts of the Middle East were beginning to be felt worldwide, and the NATO (EU) onslaught toward the steppes of Russia were now clearly visible on the world map. However, the leadership of Western democracies chooses to catalog Arab Spring or the Euromaidan, the median results were upheaval, misery, death, and the vaporizing of trust in between the principal nations involved. With the Minsk II agreements moderating the killing in the East of Ukraine, and with the refugee crisis beginning to weigh on European society, Syria and the proxy war put in place there took center stage. ISIL, the US led coalition, Russia, and Iran, and the nearly silent Israelis were all arrayed not a few miles from the citadel at Megiddo. Armageddon loomed.

I cannot remember when I was first introduced to the Romanian born artist Carmen Renieri, I only know that as @RenieriArts on Twitter she's been instrumental in disseminating the truth about the civil war in Syria. Here the story is both unique on the one hand, and similar to all the other pro-Russia actors I've met. Where Arab Spring and the chasm that Syria has become are concerned, Carmen can be classified as a foot soldier of voices influenced by Syria correspondent Vanessa Beeley.

These two characters exemplify the diversity and universalism of those who are accused of being agents of the Kremlin. And they both exhibit the same psychological profile the rest of Putin's dissidents do. Vanessa Beeley's story is coming up, but Carmen Renieri reveals her own motivations and role below.

Artists for Putin: How I Ended Up a Kremlin Troll by Carmen Renieri

Where should I begin? I started my presence on the social

media some six or seven years ago, after the gallery I successfully worked with had to close. The idea was to push my work by connecting to people interested in art.

My attempts were rather timid because I was never good at promoting myself. I tweeted quotes about art, and each new follower made me happy as I knew I need many of them to create a platform. Ha-ha! Who thought by then that I will end up posting about politics alone?

The more I was into it, the more I realized that Twitter is very political, that there are ways to fight injustice beyond joining street demos, which hardly happen here in Germany anyway.

Was I interested in politics before? Yes. But I lacked the understanding of the bigger picture.

I was born in Romania, Timisoara (1961) at a time when life was not a struggle for survival and people could afford to live a decent life, but they lacked the freedom of speech and movement.

My town is situated close to the Hungarian and ex-Yugoslavian borders and was called the "little Occident" because of its vicinity to the West. We could watch international TV from the neighboring countries and were looking with envy to the liberties they enjoyed compared to the big prison we were living in.

Nobody believed in change, so the only hope seemed to be the escape to the West, legally or illegally.

I got my first radio receiver at the age of fifteen, and I started to pull out the antenna through the kitchen window every night to listen to Radio Free Europe, back then believed by many to be the ultimate voice of truth broadcasting inside the communist bloc.

By that time, things in my country got bad. I remember my parents having to wake up at 3:00 AM to stand in queues for meat, eggs or milk before going to work, and coming home late after having to wait in other queues for similar cupboard essentials, including oil and sugar.

Other issues like electricity shortage, warm water twice a week, and hardly any heating in winter solidified the dream to go West.

RFE, BBC, and etcetera, fed my frustration. What they omitted to say was that our suffering was caused by the West, that, after courting Ceausescu with advantageous credits, they were now blackmailing him into either paying everything back under harsh austerity conditions or bowing his head.

It was years after the so-called revolution that I found out the truth about both the RFE being a CIA mouthpiece and about how the IMF pushed us into misery.

I left Romania two years before the "uprising." I first lived in Greece for a few years, then decided to come to Germany where most members of my dad´s family settled. As "ethnical Germans," we could immigrate, after years of waiting and lots of bribe money paid to middlemen who negotiated the procedure.

It was in Greece where I first saw a big demonstration. The cradle of democracy in action! I was overwhelmed by the power of masses demanding their rights with one voice. My body was shivering all over, and I started to cry.

All the years in Romania I had to give up my external liberties to preserve my inner ones.

Did I radically change after leaving my country?

I was in the West, and I was free...I thought. Not enough, as I was still caught in my own alienation and prejudiced views about the world.

Having arrived in Germany, I first swallowed the news as being truthful, just like I did with RFE in my young years. The much-respected State Media in a great democracy can impossibly lie!

Somehow, I got stuck in the naive, adolescent view that the Western society is the only one respecting human values.

I was fine with everything, I didn´t question, and I kept living my little life until the war against Yugoslavia started.

To me, Yugoslavia was the perfect compromise between socialism and the free market. I admired their system, and I was shocked and heartbroken as I saw how the Western powers were destroying it.

This war was my political awakening where I started to look behind the curtain and try to understand the unknown mechanisms and interests that lead to such a disaster.

Already then, I was confronted with accusations for "backing the criminal Serbs." I was called names, and even friends took distance from me for not swallowing the official narrative.

It is somehow sad that I feel more "at home" in the virtual world than among family and friends.

People around me don´t want to hear about carnage, famine, injustice...

Some say, "Don´t show me. It is too gruesome". Others say, "I am too little to change anything in this world."

They are wrong.

As I started to express myself on Twitter, I also felt at times there are just words in the wind until I discovered, and it made me remember the protest in Athens, that we are many speaking with one voice.

Now I am more focused and more organized trying to investigate one subject at the time. It is hard because everything is connected and the more you dig, the deeper the rabbit hole gets.

Collaborating with Vanessa taught me that conflicts are too complex as to be able to fully cover them all and that it is more important to concentrate on one card that could bring the whole house of lies to fall, just like it happened with the White Helmets.

After they were refused the Nobel Peace Prize, she told me: "Would be nice to believe" and I think she does, "that we contributed a whole lot to them being denied the award."

This gives me the confidence that we can have an impact, no matter how insignificant we are, no matter how much we are brand marked as Putinists, Assadists or conspiracy theorists. Sooner or later, truth always prevails. Without truth, there can´t be justice, without justice, there can´t be peace. Who said that? MLK?

So, this is my long journey, and I am still on my way!

Carmen Renieri

As I said, Carmen's path to the forefront of this social media free-for-all was tentative, unusual, yet in some ways typical of all of us. My wife Mihaela is from the same Romania that Carmen recounted in her contribution, and their two stories intersect at key points. While Mihaela's home in Bucharest underwent a different communism and revolution than that experienced in Timisoara, and while Carmen left the country much earlier than my wife, the truth of the West's role is evident through both their experiences.

Mihaela tells me as I write this, "What Carmen probably never knew was that Ceausescu ended up paying off all of Romania's debt". So, while other debtor nations chose to extend their debts with the IMF and other lenders, Romanians suffered austerity and paid back everything they owed[31].

Romania and Eastern Europe are in the center of Putin's chess board, Syria is at the bottom center.

On September 17, 2015, New Eastern Outlook published my article entitled "Italy's Role in a New European Disorder," in which I outlined and differentiated the relative roles of honorable military commanders from their political counterparts. Of specific note was Italian Lieutenant General Giuseppe Bernardis, whose role in the Libya regime change

---

[31]   Cornel Ban, Sovereign Debt, "Austerity, and Regime Change: The Case of Nicolae Ceausescu's Romania", in *East European Politics and Societies*, 2012 26: 743

and disdain for the business of war these days present a crystal ball view of current crises. I cited the Italian Air Force legend regarding arms sales and related military complaining. Bernardi's part in the book by the Italian Air Force, "Missione Libia 2011. Il contributo dell-Aeronautica militare" reveals Italy's part in operations Odyssey Dawn and Unified Protector, and his comments on arms dealers prove unarguably that a huge component of the Libya affair was armaments marketing. In answer to the question; "Is there a danger of Libya becoming more a marketing opportunity for aircraft than a military operation?" the general replied:

> "We are built to mount operations – we are not built for demonstrations. Le Bourget (referring to the Paris Air Show) should stay in Paris and Farnborough (UK variant) should stay in the U.K. One can start talking about being combat-proven at the end of the operation, but not during. An operation is a serious thing. [32]"

My point in bringing up General Bernardis and Italy's role in Arab Spring is to connect my "follow the money" efforts with the crises born out of militarism on the Great Game's chessboard. Libya was a continuation of the profitable war that ended with Iraq in shambles and was about to end in Afghanistan. As Obama's PR team prepared to benefit from that latter pullout, the Pentagon and Washington think tanks

---

[32] Lt. Gen. Giuseppe Bernardis Chief of Staff, Italian Air Force, interview with *Defense News*, June 6, 2011

were pleased to see the convenient villain Muammar Gaddafi being overthrown. As we see now, the destruction of the Libyan chess piece led directly to Syria moves. Bernardis is but one of many high-ranking military officers who have admitted the military industrial complex role in all the killing.

The warmongers among the military and political elite of the deep state are even more evil. If the reader can recall sound bites and memes from 2011 until now, frames of Hillary Clinton laughing about killing Gaddafi mix with the Twitter tweets of four-star *General Wesley Clark proclaiming*, "We're going to take out 7 countries in 5 years: Iraq, Syria, Lebanon, Libya, Somalia, Sudan & Iran" to drive home the dire circumstances in Syria.

The public statements of these elite politicians and militarists, along with those of their elite industrialist cronies, outline in no uncertain terms the aspiring global empire's plans for world domination.

Fast forward past the 2016 election fiasco, and more recent news from the head of the United States Central Command, General Joseph L. Votel, tells of the top command structure under President Donald Trump selling war and American boots on the ground in Syria[33]. So, the extenuation of US wars that materialized with the no-fly zone over Libya has

---

[33]   *"More U.S. Troops May Be Needed Against ISIS in Syria, a Top General Says"* by Michael R. Gordon, New York Times, February 22, 2017

not disappeared with the change of presidents.

To find out the truth, the world has looked to people like Vanessa Beeley on the ground in Syria. An honest, brave and determined witness, Vanessa unmasked the terrorist liars and infiltrators that had been evangelized and used as sources by BBC, the New York Times, and the rest of the West's mainstream media.

Why I do what I do by Vanessa Beeley

We are all being lied to on a daily if not hourly basis. The power of the apparatus producing those lies from the State aligned media, NGOs, Think Tanks and associated institutions is immense and has now infiltrated social media on a massive scale. For decades now we have been undergoing an insidious and destructive Gaslighting process, a known CIA torture procedure, designed to erode our trust in our own ability to judge situations and to determine fact from mass produced fiction.

My desire to break out of this paradigm of lies and manipulation was perhaps my primary driving factor. This is combined with a personal journey through the confidential papers and diaries of my father, Arabist, Sir Harold Beeley, middle east advisor to Ernest Bevin and British Ambassador to Cairo among other postings in the ME. The level of injustice being levied against nations that stand in the way of neocolonialism and US coalition hegemony in the ME and globally is profoundly disturbing and once witnessed or experienced, cannot be ignored and must be shouted from the rooftops, for all our sakes.

It is our duty as human beings to defend the rights of human beings worldwide to determine their own future and to protect their history, culture, and civilization from hostile, external forces that depend upon the vulnerability of these proud, honorable nations to ensure their own invulnerability worldwide.

"You cannot play with the animal in you without becoming wholly animal, play with falsehood without forfeiting your right to truth, play with cruelty without losing your sensitivity of mind. He who wants to keep his garden tidy does not reserve a plot for weeds."
Dag Hammarskjold

Our own conscience must dictate to us, the extent to which we devote our lives to combatting what threatens to ensnare us all into complicity with ethnic cleansing and mass murder being conducted by our governments against prey nations across the world.

Vanessa Beeley

Chapter XI: The Clandestine Network

"The Kremlin Trolls were never motivated by
Putin or Russia, but by the West's stupidity, and
the evil that flows from it."
Holger Eekhof

Looking back from the viewpoint of people like Vanessa Beeley, I am amazed at just how smoothly the anti-Russia narrative congealed into a global strategy and an expanded confrontation. In 2010 the "plan", if I may, began to take shape with Arab Spring spawning a series of large scale conflicts. Then the "west's" intentions for creating what amounted to a "Ukrainian Spring" became evident about the time the puppets Yulia Tymoshenko and Yuriy Lutsenko were imprisoned back in 2011 and 2012. I mention this to help the reader understand the scope and nature of our efforts to counteract the false narrative. You see, no matter how broad the view any of us has had, all the pro-Russia activism has been regional at one time or another. My own perspective is from the widest possible point of observation simply because I attempt to take it all in on a daily basis. My investigating, analysis, and reporting tends to be about "hot spots", or breaking news. But Vanessa, Graham Phillips, and most of the others are immersed in the localized conflicts, whereas The Saker, Bausman, Dr. Michel Chossudovsky at Global Research, along with me and other independents tend to bounce back and forth in efforts to contravene the globalist narrative and media/policy strategies on the broader field.

Some readers will recall the allegations that Vladimir Putin's government built a network to include all of us "trolls" and many more. I'll admit right here that part of my reason for writing this book is to show how ludicrous this assertion is. The way the "Kremlin Troll" network works is so disorganized and fluid that if Putin did create it, then he's otherworldly in his intellect and power. By way of a simple explanation, the way the journalists "source" investigators like Beeley, Phillips, and others mirrors the disconnected way in which social media works overall. In short, the dissemination of fact and opinion is far too random and situational to be orchestrated. What most people fail to understand is that social media is almost completely unpredictable. The only aspect that can be predicted at this stage, is the probability somebody will react to a given instance. As an example, if Turkey shoots down a Russian fighter plane over Syria, it's a safe bet Beeley will have some role in commenting on the fate of the pilots and that an analyst like me may "tweet" or otherwise share that comment. Among the so-called Kremlin Trolls, no one has more experience than me in either operating in, or understanding how to manipulate social media. Being an early adaptor[34] to virtually every social media platform that ever existed, I have a special understanding of how these communities operate, but more importantly how corporations, businesses, and even governments can make use of them (or even fail to). Our public relations business revolves around social media marketing, and from a professional standpoint I can tell you, corporate and

---

[34] *Phil Butler,* Search Engine Journal "About" profile page

governmental understanding and utilization of this communicative medium are infantile. There's no need to dive off into a digital media study here. The reader just needs to understand that traditional communicators are walking like pigeons in a realm they are ill equipped to control. Neither the east nor west has a good grip on the pulse of society in this regard. The method western operators use to "boost" their messages, is to throw some funding into influencer efforts. As for Russia? There is no recognizably cohesive effort, just to be honest. While there are highly skilled social media professionals working at the Ministry of Foreign Affairs of the Russian Federation or at a network like RT for instance, they are completely disconnected from one another. Furthermore, Russian media agencies may exert an overall Russia positive voice, but connectedness within these agencies is as scatterbrained as any western counterpart. This is a function of human nature and of the nature of large competitive organizations worldwide. I have numerous communiques at the highest levels that indicate this competition and even an envy in Russian media that rivals Hollywood. Any suggestion counter wise is obtuseness or an outright lie. Let me explain why.

I've already alluded to my role as a so-called "early adopter" in social media, but for the argument over Mr. Putin's alleged troll army it's important to clarify my expertise. In the early days of what became known as "Web 2.0" I was as employed by several technology media companies to test, analyze, and to report on startups like Facebook, Twitter, and a multitude of others. The short version of the story of my technology blogging days is that PR companies and even startup CEOs individually, pursued tech writers like me to report on their developments. I ended up testing and analyzing just about every startup development worth mentioning right alongside world famous tech bloggers like Michael Arrington of TechCrunch, Pete Cashmore of Mashable, ReadWriteWeb founder Richard MacManus, and the small club of now famous tech gurus. As a natural progression from this work I was later asked to join social media networks, and to later create strategies for manipulating those communities for marketing and PR purposes. In short, I became one of the world's most sought after social media experts. Later, when I joined my wife's digital PR firm, my network of colleagues and my expertise melded with her own (SEO, social media, journalism). For the purpose here, over the course of the last decade we've learned a trick or two about social media campaigns. Now, here's how this applies.

If Vladimir Putin really did organize a troll factory in St. Petersburg, Russia the Kremlin Trolls mentioned herein would have the most powerful Twitter and Facebook accounts in the world. My colleagues in Silicon Valley who helped Fortune 500 businesses leverage clients via social media will already know what I am about to tell you. For instance, a truly cohesive Twitter campaign aided by even 100 accounts can go viral in a matter of a few hours. This is particularly true if there is an ad budget behind. Now imagine my own Twitter feed the day we uncovered NATO servers being used to host a Ukraine "kill list". Instead of the two retweets my tweet on 21st April 2015 received, I'd surely have had at least 200 if St. Petersburg were online. With even 100 "operatives" aimed at the Russia Insider article "What's Behind the "Peacekeeper" Killings in Ukraine?", my extended network would have made the story a trend on Twitter. A campaign like I describe would also leverage paid tweets and the other social networks working in unison. With even a couple hundred dollars in ad money, Vladimir Putin's troll network could literally take over the message on any issue. All of this is proven marketing and PR strategy, and nothing new to the educated operator.

The pro-Russia message, much like the NATO message, is disjointed in the eyes of any expert in media manipulation. At best the efforts can be described as "grass roots" activism spurred by passive influencer efforts. The networks like RT do an expert job of maximizing their own stories, but ancillary support for other similar efforts is nonexistent just like western media outlets. Sputnik does not retweet RT stories any more than Rupert Murdoch's Wall Street Journal retweets Fox News stories. Beyond the US State Department or Ministry of Foreign Affairs of Russia news releases, competition for viewers and readers dictate more than US or Russian presidents do. The "agendas" are supported, but neither side is truly expert at disseminating truly powerful propaganda campaigns. Most of the news the world reads is "spin" in reality. An agency or influencer puts out the narrative, and the subsidiaries reiterate or outright copy the tone of voice. As for clandestine networks, the nod there has to go to the US/NATO side for the sheer force of money being expended on their message.

When the truth of which "clandestine network" is illuminated it's the NGOs backed by George Soros, the think tanks run by old Russophobes, and the entity known as the "deep state" that runs the most mechanized machine. On the opposing side, there is only Margarita Simonyan's RT media in the ring against the biggest media heavyweights on the planet. Supported by the myriad "Kremlin fans" in independent media, RT has an unbelievably loud voice. But the connection in between is intangible and very informal. Also, contrary to the way western mainstream media parrots the official Washington, London, or Brussels narrative, Simonyan's RT often picks up on independent media and journalism. Sputnik is a perfect example of this in the way reporters and writers there paraphrase and make use of analysis and information from outside sources. I'm intimately familiar with this Sputnik strategy because of calls on me for analysis, but also for the agency using reports by me at other media outlets for the purpose. Rather than simply paraphrasing or copy-pasting content, the Sputnik team creates direct news and commentary by consolidating ideas and facts[35].

Once again, Putin's supposed network of clandestine trolls has been widely used in the same way CNN was found to be boosting ratings with negative Putin news[36]. The media environment in the United States in particular show an unrepentant "fake news" ecosystem bent on traffic "no matter what". Even with media outlet after media outlet being shown misinforming, editors and journalist keep right on parroting anti-Russia rhetoric. A Business Insider author named Natasha Bertrand caught my eye in July of 2016 when

---

[35] *Riyadh's Worst Nightmare: Is Saudi Arabia's Oil Business Going Bust?*, with analysis by Phil Butler, Sputnik, November 2016

[36] *Hidden Camera Catches CNN Producer Saying Trump 'Probably Right' About Russia 'Witch Hunt'*, by Justin Caruso, The Daily Caller, June 2017

she decided to ride the wave with "It looks like Russia hired internet trolls to pose as pro-Trump Americans", regurgitating Adrian Chen's New York Times piece about the St. Petersburg "troll house"37. She also cites The Daily Beast's Michael Weiss, who's already shown is paid by not just by ousted oligarch Mikhail Khodorkovsky, but George Soros as well38. The lead in her Bertrand's article mimics all other anti-Russia diatribe I've seen in the last several years:

> *"Russia's troll factories were, at one point, likely being paid by the Kremlin to spread pro-Trump propaganda on social media."*

Bertrand's piece begins with a foregone conclusion, and the author's story ends with a quote from that is as asinine as they come. Speaking of Vladimir Putin, another young lioness journalists named Julia Ioffe is cited for her "Putin expertise" with this.

> *"All he wants is for America to see him as a worthy adversary."*

---

[37] *It looks like Russia hired internet trolls to pose as pro-Trump Americans, by Natasha Bertrand, Business Insider, July 2016*

[38] *Soros Supports Khodorkovsky Against Strengthening Russia*, KATEHON, June 2016

Ioffe was fired by Politico for a tasteless Tweet targeting at then-president elect Donald Trump, then subsequently hired by the Atlantic. The daughter of Russian-Jewish immigrants to America, the firefly Ioffe has made a career of flaming controversy. A Fulbright Scholarship recipient, the young reporter pounds the "hate Putin beat" like a drum. In my humble opinion, she's a poster child for the real clandestine media of Earth, the globalist budgeted cohorts coming from academia and the "funds" and foundations that boost journalistic and political careers[39]. Independent media has been on the case of "deep state" support for what has been termed the "Intelligence-University Complex, or a system that supports efforts like the Fulbright programs in order to create propaganda agents. [40] [41] Of course, it's impossible to know whether these intelligence community targeted students are brainwashed or selected for their predisposition toward a "message" or mission, but these agencies do coerce college students to some extent is unarguable. As for Ioffe, if the NSA or CIA did not recruit the brilliant daughter of Russian Jews who left Moscow on account of alleged anti-Semitism, they missed a stellar chance. It matters not whether these Fulbright geniuses are agents or not, for they serve the same purpose independently. My point where the Kremlin's agents in media is concerned is well made. Nobody can show the FSB funding educational opportunity for the

---

[39] Why Don't We Hear About Soros' Ties to Over 30 Major News Organizations? by Dan Gainor, Fox News, May 2011

[40] The CIA's Campus Spies, by Dave H. Price, Global Research, March 2005

41 The Intelligence-University Complex: CIA Secretly Supports Scholarships, Democracy Now, August 2005

most noted Kremlin Trolls in this book, except for my FSB Alpha Team friend, Lieutenant Colonel Stanislav Stankevich, who offers his confession in a chapter to come. Conversely, it can be shown that the US intelligence community, along with NGOs like Soros' Open Society Foundations, have sponsored academia, business, and politicians for some decades. If there is a Vladimir Putin network of trolls running amok, it's the best hidden agency ever. From inside the pro-Russia ranks all we see is vehement defense and activism, combined with organic Russia media news against an obvious smear campaign waged against Russians.

In the following chapters, I'll introduce you to the most fascinating ragtag group of truth defenders the world has ever known.

Chapter XII: My Further Confessions and Associates

"I think every person should have some faith in him, in his heart. What matters is not an external display of this faith, but the inner state of the soul."
Vladimir Putin

In this chapter, you will learn more about my comrades in the ongoing war for truth and freedom of beliefs. The following "Kremlin Troll" were either too shy or too busy to create in depth articles about their involvement, or who knows, maybe President Putin's right-hand man, Dmitry Peskov instructed them to keep things brief and tidy. Whatever their reasons for brevity and humility, I know these people well. Once again, the thread of decency that binds us together is strong, as you will deduce from more of their pull quotes. I'll present them via a brief biography and their own thoughts on being Putin fans, followed by my brief comments and admissions about them.

Levent Alver is a prolific Facebook operator and a gentle man whose parents are Alawites ("Alawi" means followers of Ali). He got involved in this media war after the Kiev supported Nazis in Ukraine killed as many as 200 innocent civilians at the Trade Union building in Odessa in 2014. In his own words below Levent sets the record straight not only for himself but for hundreds and thousands of people who understood what Odessa was about.

> *"These people were burnt to death by the EU*
> *backed Maidan supporters because they wanted*
> *a different future for their city and their country."*

I confess to an irresistible kinship with Levent both for his selfless sharing of the injustice in Ukraine, and for his innocent and good-natured support for my own and other activist's journalistic efforts.

Vera Van Horne is a Russian-Ukrainian living in Canada, a lady who makes use of her professional research and analytical skills from the financial industry, to obtain and disseminate undistorted information about geopolitical movements in the Twitter space.

> *"Before the 2014 crisis in Ukraine, I wasn't*
> *politically active at all. I mostly used mainstream*
> *and social media to follow business news and a*
> *few of my favorite journalists from Canadian and*
> *British media on Twitter. Then suddenly, during*
> *February 2014 these journalists were in Kiev*
> *covering Maidan. Since I have both Russian and*
> *Ukrainian roots, my knowledge of the people in*
> *this region, and the history and culture of both*
> *countries is rather advanced comparatively. So,*
> *when the journalists I most respected started*

writing ridiculous things about Ukrainians being oppressed from the USSR times, or when they portrayed Bandera as being a hero, a cognitive dissonance in me kicking in. Trying to restore my balance, I switched on my research skills, using my knowledge of languages, info from people on the ground and, of course, the Internet.

I also broadened the social media sources I followed to receive the information from all sides (as any decent researcher should.) I soon discovered, that unlike the written word, unedited amateur videos, uploaded by ordinary people after any development, soon became an invaluable source of "raw" data. Somewhat unexpectedly, instead of restoring my naive bubble of beliefs about the world, my research took me down the rabbit hole that I'm still descending into, and it's not a happy place.

Discovering that the so-called "mainstream media" is not an unbiased, truthful source of information, but a heavily-controlled network that tirelessly creates what you thought was reality is an uncomfortable truth. To realize that your "freedom of speech" can carry the heavy price of being blacklisted as a radical, joining a long list of war veterans and journalists, who were fired for not "reporting" according to the orders of their superiors is a stunning revelation. As for becoming a Kremlin troll, like someone said, it's easy - all you must do is start telling the truth."

My confession here is that I know more about Vera's plight than I am willing to disclose and that she is a soldier for good in the world, that above all else.

Christoph Heer joined Twitter back in 2012, which was before Ukraine was torn apart. A piano teacher who lives in Switzerland, Christoph's first Tweet about me concerned an article I wrote for Russia Insider, and it read *"Your words to God's ears."* This betrays the man's reasoning for becoming a "Kremlin Troll." The following paragraph lets us know why he raised his voice in dissent in 2014.

> *"I consider myself thoroughly apolitical. I may be a philosopher, but most of all I just love God and spend my free time in meditation. I joined twitter to follow and support Valentina Lisitsa. She has my utmost respect and admiration. My "work" on twitter grew naturally and intuitively. I love the company of truth tellers and still enjoy the vast richness of available information, and I'm committed to support and defend the great work of truth tellers on twitter. And so, it happened that my twitter activity became appreciated (while I'm blocked by great many). My motto might be: Truth is worth the effort to spread news from a vast variety of sources and intelligent commentators. I didn't search the fight, but once I realized to what extent MSM are lying, I welcomed the fight wholeheartedly. IMHO, I have a DUTY to counteract the lies. The deeper problem may be the masses who welcome being manipulated and, to be honest, I doubt we can have a significant impact on that. But I don't want to change the world. A tiny, individual, contribution is enough for me."*

My further confession is that I share many of Christoph's views including the critical role Israel and Zionist interests are playing a huge role in all this upheaval of late.

John Delacour has been labeled a "Top 10 Kremlin Troll" (#9) for his dissenting view on Ukraine, Russia, and the Syria catastrophe. Here is his story in his own words.

"Born on the day the Russians liberated Auschwitz, I grew up to read Chinese at Cambridge (1964-8), during which time the middle the Cultural Revolution began. I later taught English as a foreign language in Italy, France, and England till 1976 and, with the end of the Cultural Revolution, was finally invited to teach in Shanghai. I spent two years there, arriving 6 months before the death of Mao Zedung and witnessing the changes as the Deng Xiaoping faction consolidated its power. On my return from China and set up shop as a piano maker/restorer. I joined Twitter in early 2014 and became interested in the Ukraine/Donbass situation, particularly about the barrage of false narrative or anti-Russian news. I followed the Russians to Syria in September 2015 and have since specialized in the Syrian war as the starting point for a grand shift in the axis of power in the world. While I closely watching developments on the ground and at the international level, I take special interest in the manipulation of opinion by governments and the press using an unprecedented output of disinformation, fakery, and fraud. In the end, I look forward to a day when the perpetrators of these crimes can be quickly exposed, prosecuted and punished under new popular judicial procedures."

Tatiana Pahlen (aka TatianaNY) is a poet, writer, illustrator, and cartoonist, and owing to a beautify, charm and intelligence, something of the socialite on the Manhattan social scene. Tatiana joined Twitter back in 2011 and took up the banner for Russia about the same time as the rest of us. The following pull quote from a recent conversation between us puts in perspective "the westerners" including Germany's Angela Merkel, Petro Poroshenko, and what I have loving come to refer to as the "western oligarchs:"

> *"So, because these thirsty vampires, longing for their vanished youth, they would rather welcome the wreckage and total destruction of the places they used to live, even for a short lifespan. By conquering them, they eradicate their own past."*

I confess to being amazed at the number of famous people Tatiana knows who frequent NYC. High society and the political, philosophical, even artistic elites. She's prolific in a way most so-called NATO trolls will never grasp.

Greg Galloway is another prominent social media voice often referred to as either a Kremlin or Putin troll. I've been connected to Greg (aka @NewsCoverUp) the last couple of years. When I asked him about his motivation for chiming in on the anti-Russia nonsense, here's what he Tweeted me back:

> *"The mass killings of civilians in Odessa, and later in the whole of the Donbass got me seriously upset and compelled me NOT to remain silent. The MH17 and Syrian tragedies later got me even more committed... I simply cannot remain idle while during my lifetime such widespread massacres occur. Events in my personal*

life seem dwarfed by the scope of the human drama and tragedies unfolding under our very eyes."

I confess that I have depended on Greg for social media support for my own research, stories, and ideas over the last few years. Like so many, he is always supportive on top of being informative on the real stories from the Donbass and Syria.

Enrico Ivanov, also known as @Russ_Warrior, is another prominent pro-Russian operative on Twitter. A historian, teacher, and archeologist, Enrico is not actually his real name, but his dedication to finding out and revealing the truth of this Cold War II mess is reflected in his tweets, and in this comment, he gave me:

"I decided to join this battle because I always liked geopolitics and I understood that Russia wasn't the aggressor in all this. So, I wanted to fight against the Orwellian reality of the mainstream media."

Enrico is one of the most interesting of my Kremlin Troll comrades, I readily admit to admiring him for his ability to cut to the chase when the bullshit and lies of the globalists come into the light.

Maria Engström is an IT professional and a property caretaker who is as dedicated as anyone to the cause of peace. An agent of Putin, she even bought herself her very own Kremlin Troll T-shirt not so long ago. The Swedish conservative who says her country has been destroyed by flaming liberals has been along for the pro-Russia ride ever since Ukraine exploded.

"Following the war against Libya and Syria, and later also the Ukrainian civil war, I quickly noticed that what was reported in the western mainstream media had very little to do with the reality - after talking with people actually living in these places this only got more obvious. To be able to look at myself in the mirror, sleep with a good conscience and feeling good about handing over the world to the next generation I could not just watch the western world burn our planet, destroy nations, kill millions of people, all for greed, power, and geopolitics. I had to speak out, western colonial mindset needs to be challenged, and the horrible consequences of it must come to an end before it's too late. One great country that I feel is challenging this is Russia, with its foreign policy it seeks to establish a multipolar world, thanks to the Russian intervention in Syria and Crimea's vote and consequently safe return to the motherland we now have that multipolar world. I have nothing but respect and love for Russia that did not only saved Europe from Nazism in the 1940s but also saved us from a unipolar world in the 2000s. I'm appalled about the demonization and misrepresentation of Russia and President Vladimir Putin in the western mainstream media. Therefore, I'm a 'Kremlin troll'..."

While I was working with Charles Bausman and the team at Russia Insider I became acquainted with many of the most determined and dedicated pro-Russia activists. **Dmitry Zolotarev** was one of the most enthusiastic, a contributor and translator who also unearthed a ton of counter narrative.

Dmitry is a linguist, journalist, and sportsman who was branded a " Kremlin Troll" very early on by A. Weisburd.

"Russia has been targeted by Western media since forever, even as far back as 200 years ago. It matters not if we are talking about communist Russia, Peter the Great's era, or the administration of Vladimir Putin. For the media there is ALWAYS something to be afraid of, and there's ALWAYS something to splash on paper, even if the news is groundless conjecture.

So, Russian society has gotten used to and has been always prepared to things like that. Each time a new anti-Russia narrative arrives, Russia is forced to opposes new media bites by first learning, and then reinventing methods for counteracting. The only thing that has really changed is how technical progress and methodology affect messaging. New technical resources allow Media companies to create and stage anything, even that which never happened.

Today the media can orchestrate anything to make it appear as another "threat coming from Russia" and which general society will willingly bite into. Only for the last two decades have Russian journalists been trained in these new technologies, and only in the last few years have popular media outlets like RT and Sputnik arisen to deliver a true information and counter-narrative to the world.

I believe WE are now more successful in this media war, do you know why? Because Russia uses REAL FACTS, while Western Media delivers on thin air. Real Facts are TANGIBLE THINGS, and NOTHING can beat the TRUTH."

At the start of this Putin fanboy confessional I introduced

you to a real genius, and a man or conviction and faith affectionately referred to as The Saker. Andrei (his given name) is the perfect example of conviction to the cause of truth about Russia. I am sure no one in our midst would argue here. However, with so many extraordinary and deep down good people involved in this nasty business of information warfare, I'll admit having some difficulty in choosing the Kremlin Troll best suited to end this book. That is until I remembered my good friend Paul Payer.

Paul lives in Germany these days. A former captain in the US Army Ordnance Corps 1983 – 1993, Paul served during Operation Provide Comfort in 1991, which was a mission to defend Kurds fleeing their homes in northern Iraq in the aftermath of the Gulf War. Though he'd hesitate himself to blame his debilitating lung disease (COPD) on exposure to chemical weapons in Iraq, I'm here to suggest his service cost him years of life. But Paul's sacrifice and service during the first Gulf War are not what I admire most about him. His devout Orthodox faith and his dogged pursuit of the truths about Russia are. Here is a part of Paul's unusual story.

How I Got a Life - Paul Joseph Payer

When Twitter was still relatively new, I decided that since it would take a while to get my own commercial site up offering web design ready, I decided to concentrate on promos for human rights issues to do a bit of good while learning how to conquer social media.

I focused mainly on Iran, and other spots where I thought

fundamental rights were infringed upon both in law, and how against whom (in an equal protection sense) laws were enforced. Soon, I found myself having to tweet about the worst violations, happening in nations that were allies of the US especially in the "War on Terror." Saudi Arabia comes most to mind.

Around the time I had the framework for that setup and expanding my tweets, I also indulged my love of creativity, promoting Indi musicians, actors, etc. mixed in with mega hits to generate interest. I also met some that had been A-Listers when I was growing up, honing my skills by working on a friendship/fan basis on Twitter with Mark Lane, Tony Tarantino, Adrienne Barbeau and a few others, and made some lovely friendships. Meeting Bill Zucker though is what took my endeavors into the Promotional Big League. An entertainer on the old Kelsey Grammer Todd HD site, and famous for the TARP song, we met while he was doing a live concert online in Lydia Cornell's living room of all places. We hit it off and decided to conquer Twitter together, he already with over 100,000 followers. Many a night we would knock heads developing, testing, then honing strategies; to include quick talks in between sets during his live concerts. By the end of it all, at his passing, Billy had just shy of 1 million followers (half of which were deleted by twitter when they started suppression of accounts for business and political reasons), and I had achieved an exposure of well over 12 million accounts per day. Bill himself was never political, stuck to entertainment and the occasional charity. I was about to become extremely political.

At this time, Russia was also a fascination. At the fall of the Soviet Union, while still in the military, I had studied the Tsar and any new info I could find. I was enthralled by the rise of the Orthodox Church once again, in its journey to become a lynch pin once again of Russian society. I almost broke my ribs laughing though when I'd read that the Church had glorified the last Tsar and family as Saints. So, I researched it, re-reading among others Dr. Sutton, the newest cross-referenced findings out of the old Soviet Archives, Russian and then General Eastern Orthodox Church history and doctrine, etc.

About half way through I made the decision to convert to Orthodoxy and the Holy Royal Martyrs Romanov are among my most revered Saints.

As the quality of press reporting continued to degrade to the point of almost pure propaganda and black out, and as the courts neutralized more and more of the US Constitution, coupled with we (US) morphing from fighting terror to starting wars of Empire, more and more my task was getting out accurate information and to combat the now continual war mongering propaganda. It was no longer just a matter of human rights, but of the preservation of what was left off, and that someday, reinstatement of the Constitutional Protections that had made the US Republic unique and exceptional.

South Ossetia, the clear start of a war, actually bombing Russian Military Peace Keepers there by treaty, was a good background from the recent past ... the so-called Color Revolution blueprint, of course, being the overthrow of the Tsar and shown with original documentation presented, by Dr. Sutton.

Ukraine, the violent over throw of a democratically elected government, murder and rape in ODESSA while the MSM cheered, outright easily seen thru lies by State Dept., MSM and the govt to include POTUS.   Ethnic cleansing of the Russian speaking population that had been there since the 9th Century and had been the clear majority there since the 18th.

Hillary Clinton's famous "We came, we saw, he died" after the murder and rape of Gadhafi .. and opening the once nation of Libya into a mish mash of areas mostly controlled by ISIS.

Gen. Clark's revelations of "our allies" founding, funding, and training ISIS to take out Hezbollah, itself founded, funded, and trained to take out the PLO by Mossad.

Because of the absolute incompetence of the US occupation of Iraq, making the need for another war inevitable once ISIS was unleashed on the now Shia rulers of Iraq.

My strategy or types of tweets never really changed in as the US lost more and more of its Republic, and increased the intensity of the wars of Empire. I would research the claims, call out lies or inaccuracies and tweet the facts. Apparently, this made me a Putin troll. It got to the point, especially regarding Ukraine, that I would only call it a day tweeting, once I had received so many death threats, as then I could be assured that I had done my job.

Also as the years went by, the destruction of the US as a Republic was becoming more and more clear. Court rulings weakening some and then almost all aspects of constitutional protections, self-imposed news blackouts, and outright propaganda, CNN selling infomercials presented as news to the highest US Ally bidder, the rise of the Deep State to unprecedented power and for the first time for all practical purposes, rule.

And of course, in my opinion, the reason (working with ISIS / Al Qaida) of Sens McCain, Graham, Rubio, Sec Clinton, Kerry, President Obama, etc. ... and the latest; the sitting heads of intelligence agencies and cabinet departments working in the open to take down the elected President of The United States.

Only truly free exchanges of perspectives and accurate information and news can thwart the endless bloodletting of Imperial wars, and lead to the restoration of some semblance of justice and restoration of the Republic. Only these will stop the blood-letting now going on, and the deaths of so many including the now into the millions martyred Christians – the most since Mao's executions, the attempts to destroy a now free and with the moral values of a Christianized, Russia. A Russia whose values have now come to reflect those of the working-class Americans in the 50s and 60s to include the religious, and those of a striving for liberty, but in the context of Russian culture. The war mongering and outright attacks against her are for the sole reason for fear of economic competition, and the loss of trillions to some back home in deep state war profits. Russia grows because she largely implements the domestic policies that the United States used to, before the Petro Dollar and FED deficit spending.

The wars of Racism, Empire, and Economics, formerly attempted by the Fascists and Communists past, this time done, for all intents and purposes by our US neocons both left and right, in the name of peace and tolerance, while all the while nurturing and using the brutal murderers of organizations such as ISIS.

Witnessing the video of the walk thru in the aftermath of the Odessa Massacre, the rape, execution, and burning alive of children; against such heartless atrocity I will NEVER back down. This destruction of the US Republic and the unleashing of such brutality on the world cannot be allowed to stand.

That is why I am a Putin Troll.

222

Chapter XIII: Blown

"So obscure are the greatest events, as some take for granted any hearsay, whatever its source, others turn truth into falsehood, and both errors find encouragement with posterity."
Tacitus, The Annals of Imperial Rome

When I finally set out to write about the people involved in defending Russia against the unjust lies of Western governments and media, I swore to myself, my wife, and my children I would reveal the absolute truth as I know it. From the onset of my involvement, I feared that my idealism would at some point run headlong into a pointy spear of reality. Now, at the end of the journey I wear my rusty Don Quixote suit with pride in knowing I've helped reveal the truth of Putin's digital soldiers. The unembellished Kremlin Troll story reveals that even shiny armor can't protect an impure heart. Even inside brotherhood of pro-Russia support there are those with mercenary intentions. Opportunists emerge from every good intentioned fight in either western or eastern culture. Time and pressure exert a strong influence on us, after all, and some of my colleagues in this war of dissent fell prey to the same old capitalist philosophies. In the battle against a catastrophic globalist scheme to unhinge Russia, fame and the promise of enumeration caused some so-called "Kremlin Trolls" to wander. This is the diplomatic way of saying that some really good Putin agents sold out in the same way our western media caved in. Journalists and broadcast people, academics and idealists, some of the mightiest voices for sanity lost sight of their original reasoning. They became victims of the same covetous beast that powered western mainstream media – self-interest. But these wayward Kremlin Trolls are few and far in between. The reader has already read about the most infamous Putin defenders right here in these pages. I mention these wayward sold only so that you can grasp the reality of the pro-Russia fight. Of the two or three hundred who took on the western media empire, only a handful became slaves to their newfound fame and fortune. So, compared to traditional media and activism in America, for instance, the pro-Russian side is not near so convoluted.

The most iconic Russia agents are here in full view. The people presenting their confessions in this book are emblematic of a few more who chip away day in and day out, battling the biggest lie in history. But there is one final cohort of Putin warriors I've yet to adequately profile – the genuine Russian comrades, men, and women who blow my cover as a Kremlin operative. Real hard-core Russians like my dear friend, Vladimir Vladimirovich Samarin, are the real reason for my fight. Once you read his story, and the story of my FSB comrade Stas, you'll have a window into the soul of Russia, and the people we Kremlin Trolls rushed forward to defend.

V Means Vladimirovich or "My Life in Too Few Words"

According to my Birth Certificate, I was born on October 5, 1970, in Moscow. I don't remember the fact exactly, so I have no other choice as to believe the document. My Dad Vladimir T. Samarin (then 25 — way younger than I am now) worked then as an interpreter at the building of Aswan Dam in Egypt and decided I must be born in Moscow. It was very wise of him — him, being born in London in 1945.

I remember myself since about 1975. My remembrances of the time are sweet and bright. And not only because the grass was greener then, and trees were higher, and my beloved parents were young, jolly and active. It was the time of worldwide hopes. It was the year of the EPAS program, which connected an Apollo with a Soyuz way above the Earth — and it was a true challenge for the both countries: even the atmosphere on the spaceships differed greatly, and it took both the USA and the USSR more than two years of hard work to settle everything and make the ships 'compatible'.

It was the year of Helsinki Accords — and Europe thought for aa while, that black pages of the WWI and WWII are over, forever.

I remember the very optimistic atmosphere of the time — I knew already I lived in the very best country in the world, and the world itself was firmly going to be better and better. And now I am a bit afraid that those who missed the time could call me a liar — but it had been just like I said. If there was a worldwide optimism at least once, it was in 1975.

In 1977, I went to school — a Soviet school, which undoubtedly was a part of the world's best Soviet educational system. Just like millions of my compatriots, soon I became an Octoberite. Then — a young Pioneer, with that sacredly red scarf on my neck. And at 14 I was immensely proud to become a Komsomol (Soviet YCL) member.

Meanwhile, at 10 I started to learn English. I cannot say I gained some great success in the subject at school, but heritage, evidently, worked: my Dad was a highly skilled interpreter and translator, my Mom was a school teacher of English, my Granddad also spoke English good enough to work (well, rather serve, for he was a Red Army major, then colonel-lieutenant, an air force assistant to the Soviet military attaché) in London since 1943 till 1949.

Coming to my late teens, the difference between the taught ideology and existing life became more and more evident for me. Anyhow, I was an optimist still, and evidently a bit too much: I failed to enter the Moscow University right after the school, at 17.

Being jobless was a crime in the USSR. I can spell it: being jobless for 3 months and more was a crime that could lead to an imprisonment. Yes: it was a country that had some job for everyone (let alone some dwelling, some general education and some medical service — all those things you might consider communist propaganda and as such a lie; and wrongly so).

And I had a fantastic year working for the Moscow State Committee of the State Statistics. It did help me to understand things better, but still more useful became the fact that I failed at my 2nd try to enter the MSU. Now that I became 18, I had to go to Army.

And it was quite an experience. I started with 5 months of learning in a unit located in the Ukraine, and. having become a skilled specialist in electric devices of fighter planes, I was dispatched to a unit in Soviet Latvia.

All that was great not because I had a chance to seen various places, but because in our men only collectives I had to get along with representatives of (almost) all the Soviet ethnicities: Western Ukrainians, Latvians, Lithuanians, Estonians, Kazakhstanis, Kyrghizstanis, Azeris, Armenians — just to name a few (a few — for just in Russia alone there are about 250 ethnicities). Some of them were of Moslem background, some — of Buddhist, some — of Catholic, etc.

Sociologically, the USSR was an empire just like the former Russian Empire had been — but not because of those invented by Western propaganda, Soviet totalitarianism or whatever other ideological bullshit you called it. Just because it was a country that united peoples of various religious descendance. It's that simple.

It was a strange time when I returned home, end of 1990. The country was seemingly collapsing, but I was young, and I had a task: to enter the University. And my parents had jobs, and I had not enough time to judge what happened. I made it to the Preparation Faculty, and thus secured my entering the 1st course a year later.

Which started in a different country. 1991 was a year of

clearance. In March, we had a peak of direct democracy — our referendum on the keeping the USSR. And less than half a year later it was flushed down a toilet, proving that democracy is just a word.

Demography is a bitch. It shows that the cost of the disintegration of the USSR just for the Russian Federation was at least 12 million people — including my Father. He could survive his CRF, and he survived 5 heart attacks (well, the Soviet medicine was not that bad). But his second stroke killed him.

The trouble is, I was old enough to remember the USSR when the country collapsed. And I am educated enough to see and understand, what was good then, and what is bad now (admittedly, and vice versa).

However, for those of the so-called intelligentsia and even more so-called liberals, it's unacceptable to say good things neither about bad old Soviet Union, not about bad now existing Putinite Russia.

I don't want my country to lose all those good things achieved at the 'red' time; I don't want my country to lose all those good things that are now.

It's more than enough (for some) to call me all possible names, including a Stalinite, an old Soviet Fart, a Commie, an Internationalist, a Putinite, a Kremlin troll, etc.

However, being a father myself now (my beautiful sons now

are 25 and 19), I don't feel like keeping silence.

I feel like I have a right to give things names as well. It's my country; it's my history (and that of my family); it's my small world and Earth. Just like yours — and if we want our children to survive us, we must talk and reach agreements. We must remember history so that not to repeat life threatening mistakes, and try to improve things that could lead us to a better life.

As it was in the beginning, is now, and ever shall be.

Amen.

English Matters

I was lucky enough to get a decent economy education in the College of Afro-Asian Studies of the Moscow State University, still strengthened by my passion for reading cognitive books.

And not only in Russian; following steps of my Granddad, Dad and Mom, I gained quite a good command of English, supported by a certain level of Afrikaans, German and some others.

I didn't need much time to understand that Russophobic and anti-Russian propaganda had been reigning across mainstream Western media at least since the 16th century, just like anti-Russian sanctions, which can be traced down to at least 1548.

People in Europe (and later in the USA) got so accustomed to the powerful stream of defamatory misinformation and disinformation about Russia that the media didn't have to spend much effort trying to pervert the Communist ideology under which Bolsheviks tried to make my country the best one in the world.

But that were not Bolsheviks who made the 20th century the bloodiest for my homeland. It was not they who initiated the bloody Civil War. Neither did they start the foreign intervention of the powers trying to overthrow the Bolshevik rule or at least bite some parts of weakened Russia here or there. The UK (together with Australia, Canada, and India), France, Italy, Greece, Romania, the USA sent their troops to young Soviet Russia. So did Japan. So did countries of the beaten in WWI Central Powers, first of all, Germany. Even newly born Finland used its chance to kill the Red (though, the latter did not bother much dividing the White from the Red; they preferred to kill all Russians. Now some Finnish nationalists say the Princedom of Finland within the Russian Empire was way more independent than now, within the EU; but that's now).

Then, we were made to face the aggression of the European Union 2.0 (taking the Napoleonic version for the first one). They stupidly say it was Molotov-Ribbentrop Pact that allowed Hitler to unleash the WW2 — skillfully disregarding all the efforts of the USSR made since about 1934 (by the way, in that year Poland became the first country to make an agreement with Hitlerite Germany) to build up a system of collective safety in Europe. Stalin sought a safety accord with the UK and France till August 1939 but was literally pissed off by the powers.

Well, it's a long story of lies, bullshit, betrayals and the stuff, which lasts till now. Just some examples.

Reading the well-known book "A Relation or Memorial Abstracted out of Sir Jerom Horsey's Travels..." (printed in London first early in the 1600-s) we learn that in 1570 Tsar Ivan IV (the Terrible) came to Novgorod with an army of 30,000 of Tartars (!) and 10,000 Oprichniki, that killed there 700,000 men, women and children.

A terrible blood-thirsty tyrant, isn't he? Well, he was not soft and kind, but all the population of Novgorod was 30 to 40 thousand people at the time. And the city was suffering from a plague epidemic. The personal death-bill of Ivan IV counted about 2800 people; the full dead count could reach 5000. Is it much? Yes, it is. Does it make Ivan IV the Terrible? No, in no case; European monarchs of Britain or/and France were WAY more bloodthirsty.

This was about 450 years ago. How does it go now? It goes the same way.

A review at The Guardian[42] (or lies – which for the matter

---

[42] *Russian war film set to open amid controversy over accuracy of events,* The Guardian, by Shaun Walker, November 23, 2016

coincides now), regarding the movie "Panfilov's 28" professes:

> *"Arguments over the upcoming film and the mythology around the episode, in general, began last spring, when Sergei Mironenko, the director of Russia's state archive, gave an interview stating that while there had indeed been a bloody battle outside Moscow, it was not as many had understood it.*
>
> *His words provoked such outrage that over the summer the archive posted online a 1948 internal Soviet military report into the events, which came to the conclusion that a journalist from the Red Army's newspaper had made up the particulars of the story, inventing quotes and ignoring the fact that some of the soldiers had survived and one was believed to have surrendered to the Germans.*
>
> *The legend was cooked up to fit in with the Soviet demand that soldiers should fight to the death rather than surrender.*
>
> *Vladimir Medinsky, the culture minister, reacted furiously to the intervention, saying it was not the job of archivists to make historical evaluations, and if Mironenko wanted to change professions, he should do so. Shortly after, Mironenko was fired."*

One can conclude that the imperial culture minister, a sub of the evil deity of Putin, fired a fair archive officer. No doubt, any non-Russian speaking human being would agree. And fail: for 1) Mr. Mironenko many times was caught hot lying about our history, and 2) he was retired for having reached the limit age of a state officer, which is 65 years. Moreover, he remained the scientific administrator of the State Archive, and is that now.

Fuck them all.

Call me names, call me a Kremlin troll or whoever, but so far as I live, I won't keep silent. I am going to deliver the truth.

And fuck the bullshit.

Vladimir Vladimirovich Samarin

My friend Vladimir Samarin lives not too far from the Kremlin and Red Square. As my friend and a subject in my book he also hints at another real motivation for my own vehement support for Russia. Despite his "Soviet" military past though, Vladimir is one of those "ordinary" citizens who step up to become heroes of a war or movement. He's another of the fascinating people who came from out of nowhere to do battle with the most expensive media empire the world has ever known. They are ordinary people on the one hand, and extraordinary on the other.

But if any of my Russian friends really "blows" my cover, it's a real Kremlin operative, my good friend Lieutenant Colonel Stanislav Stankevich. Stas, as I refer to him, is a former member of Spetsgruppa "A", also known as **Alpha** Group, an elite, stand-alone sub-unit of Russia's special forces.

The following is a translation of his own words on this new Cold War we find ourselves mired in.

Russian Vets Say: "Hey, We Are NOT Trolls!"

At some stage, any person thinks about the meaning of his life and often finds this meaning in the struggle for what he believes. For example, in preventing new wars and creating a just world in which there is a place for any people, nation, religion, a way of life.

What are the wars for? To satisfy the commercial interests of individuals who have no homeland, no soul, no conscience, and all their actions in this world assessing by the mathematical attitude of the profits to risk.

Any president, king, or even a dictator depends on the opinion of his people. In a democratic society, deputies and parliamentarians are also forced to rely on the view of the electorate, and no decision on war can be taken without the participation of the people. After all, those who go to war with weapons in their hands or send their children to it must support such a decision, or soon they will oppose those who sent them.

How do modern wars begin? First, an image of the evil enemy is created, and for this everything that is associated with the opponent is painted in dark colors, he is shown unpredictable and bloodthirsty. At the same time, access to information that could break this idyllic picture is blocked. After a while, one can bravely start a war in which there will have support and sacrifice of the people who do not even guess about real goals of this war.

How the USSR Lost the Cold War

In the Soviet Union and in the United States in the late 1940s to early 1990s, this mechanism for creating an image of an enemy worked well. The USSR had many advantages over the United States, but there were also many cons. Hollywood and Mosfilm produced terrible movies from their opponents on the other side of the Iron Curtain. Capitalists brought up in the laws of the market successfully sold Hollywood movies and Coca-Cola in beautiful tins all around the world, while the USSR could not boast of its information goods with its Spartan, calm, multinational and traditional philosophical way of life. Against this background, Gorbachev betrayed all information positions of his country. The Soviet Union suddenly became a villain even in the eyes of its citizens, but at the same time, everything that was done in the West became an example of humanity, justice, success and role models.

The peoples of the former USSR rushed into the arms of the brothers from the US and Europe, who brought them light and a loaf with a traditional Russian outlet, called a "hamburger." We had bread loaves with cutlets before, even healthier and tastier, but could these meals compare with those in a beautiful packaging imposed on us in outlandish advertising?

It took years, famine, wars and the disgrace of predatory privatization (the initial accumulation of capital, as Karl Marx would say) so that people would wake up and realize that they are still at war with the enemy who has the goal of destroying their state, the nation and the people, seizing wealth and territory of the country. And the most horrible and insulting thing is that the citizens of the USSR, by their own naivety and stupidity, turned their lives into humiliation and shame with elements of despair, allowed the crooks to seize power over themselves, and a handful of scammers to steal their people's wealth during privatization.

Just think, the peoples of the USSR as children were meeting the American brothers, and now they hear in the new Hollywood movies and media interviews the bragging of the heroes of the US victory in the Cold War. Americans even issued a medal with the appropriate title, which, of course, was awarded to Mikhail Gorbachev.

In any case, the position of the USSR in the information war was weaker than the position of the United States. During the entire period of the Cold War, the Soviet State blackened the enemy, and was also forced to prevent the penetration of information from the West into the country's territory, including suppressing the of broadcasts of "Voices", not letting its citizens abroad, and, in the end, USSR has lost.

The Turning-point

> *"Who does not regret the collapse of the USSR,*
> *he does not have a heart. And the one who*
> *wants to restore it in its former form does not*
> *have a head."*
> *Vladimir Putin*

But, what do we have now? As in any war, the USSR was waging in its territory, we retreated long and painfully, bearing heavy losses and gaining experience and strength. From the beginning of the 2000s, the situation began to change dramatically. We saw a path that could be taken in the creation of a new state if we did not submit to another's will. We understood that could absorb all the best from the West, integrate into the world community without humiliation, wars, human sacrifices and the disintegration of a great country, which became the greatest tragedy for millions of people in the entire former Union.

The 21st century came - the information age. We suddenly realized and accepted for the rule that information no longer knows the boundaries, and the Internet does not allow to continue to live, dividing the world into zones of information influence.

Previously, politicians did not bother to explain to the people the reasons for their decisions - they limited themselves to simplified versions that left many delicate nuances in the background. Now, these invented simple versions immediately fall under the stream of criticism from the other side, are being questioned, broken, and, finally, turning against the one who invented them.

Before, the state could poke a finger at a neighbor, condemn it, say that it must be punished and get support for its actions. It does not work anymore. And it will never work again. But it seems that while the US State Department is still trying to understand this, Russia skillfully uses the new information landscape to achieve tactical advantages.

Vladimir Putin, from the first days of his work as President of Russia, understood that it was necessary to clarify his decisions, not to lie and not to leave the answers. A few years later, his open style of communication and many hours of speaking to journalists on the air have become a norm. He is friendly to many opponents because he is not afraid, to tell the truth. He is free in his decisions because he can hear and agree with the opposition without prejudice to his image, as he can discuss his decisions publicly from the point of benefits for the people even complicated for understanding.

A good leader is not one who is always right, but one who created a system that unites different people who think differently and have a wide variety of competencies and experience around a single goal. It is in the variety of thoughts surrounding us that we develop sound ideas that can improve our lives. I vote in the election of Vladimir Vladimirovich Putin because the system he created allows Russian citizens to disagree with the government, to think in the way they want, and at the same time feel protected, to be a part of this society working for the benefit of own family and own country.

Comparing how elections in the US and Russia are held, what unimaginable and hypocritical claims the loser party makes to the new American president and our country, I understand that over the past three decades, Russia has become the leader of democratic freedoms, leaving the US far behind. And all the hysteria of the media and officials in the West look like a babble of an offended schoolboy who can no longer be considered the best in the class. I would like this schoolboy to draw conclusions and begin to pull himself up to excellent classmates, and not once came to school with a .223 caliber, indiscriminately shooting pupils and teachers.

This terrible Russian propaganda

War and politics are dirty work, and, as one of my little friend, said, "The princesses go to the toilet too." I am far from thinking that our policy is an exception to the rules, and it smells like flowers, but when reading the English-language and Russian-language press, everyone can notice that, in fact, Russia's actions are stronger, more honest and more humane, then often the foul-smelling newsbreaks from the transatlantic "The bulwark of democracy".

The main thing that catches the eye is that Russia looks in all the media like a country living under the international law, by the arrangements, and the US increasingly manifests itself as a hooligan, a madcap, who violates the rules established by him because now those roles increasingly prevent them.

In order not to lie, you must be decent. Previously, politics needed to walk in expensive suits, make a smart face and not catch the eye of journalists, while having fun in expensive brothels. And now, in the age of Assange and WikiLeaks, one should behave well, even when no one seems to see it. Western politicians are not ready for this. Most of them are still trying to hide or veil the reasons for their decisions, they express their opinions in public and take actions that they really disagree with.

Russian media are often accused of bias. Can someone else believe in free journalism that does not depend on the roles of the market? It would be strange if the news agencies funded by State or any other party focused on judgments of the opponents.

At the same time, Russian media have an advantage over their Western counterparts. For a long time, the Russian press has not hesitated to cover the opposite point of view, to submit hot, even unpleasant news on the pages of federal publications to take the initiative into their own hands, telling about the opponent's position with the simultaneous opposition of his own. At the same time, the journalist is given a chance to disclose his opinion in all variegated colors - that is what I see, what surprises and delights me as a reader.

Therefore, I personally am more impressed by the position of Russian media than the New York Post or the Wall Street Journal, which print a one-sided delusion, calculated that the consumer of information will never see the arguments of opponents. In one studio or one Russian federal edition, I can find out everything that concerns the issue, without resorting to studying the sites of opponents to clarify the whole picture.

Although, in all honesty, I am tired of seeing every evening on Russian federal channels the dominance of Ukrainian and American political scientists.

I would like to dwell on the CNN channel, which the US people consider almost the main friend and lawyer of Russia. The abbreviation CNN stands for the Cable News Network, but the familiar Americans since the time of the Soviet Union have been deciphering this name with humor as the Communist News Network. In fact, I would compare CNN with our "Echo of Moscow," but CNN is much more modest in its oppositional judgments than its Russian counterpart. Let me express my opinion that for Russia to have such a friend as CNN anyway, is like to have a gay cobber. You never know when, and why he makes you blush.

Russians and Americans, what makes us different?

I tried to find out through reading the threads of discussion in social networks, who mostly call to wars and to crusades in the US and in Russia? Those who know about the war only by hearsay. I do not consider those who harbor personal grievances, earn in war, or both, as a pilot John McCain shot down by Soviet soldiers in Korea. I do not consider those who are already under threat of destruction - the people of Yemen, Syria, the East of Ukraine as well.

Communicating with my friends Americans and British in social networks, I concluded that veterans on both sides of the ocean who were holding weapons on the battlefield, who understand the whole black warfare essence, are always ready to defend their country and loved ones, they frightfully routinely hold their guns under the pillows and pray for never having to use them in combat. Paradoxically, even when we are on different sides of the barricades, we find a common language with each other faster than many other people.

Although there is the difference also. We have fundamentally different upbringing - We in Russia are shameless and straightforward, they are polite and discreet. We perceive our combat experience as a collective work, while they do like a competition of individuals. Our professionals do not tell, especially publicly about how the villains were killed, because they perceive this as a forced measure, evil, and the Americans veterans regularly tell about their murders, are proud of this. If we traditionally preach indulgent attitude towards the defeated enemy, then the Internet is full of photos from Abu-Grave, stories of mockeries of prisoners of war, contempt for the lives of civilians as a collateral damage. It's understandable, we were brought up in the movie "They fought for their country," and Americans grew up with Sylvester Stallone as Vietnam Green Beret "Rambo," John J.

But Americans do not consider themselves villains. They also have kindness and humanity, and we have much in common, which should unite us rather than disunity. We are afraid only of those whom we do not understand.

Many Russians see Americans as unintentional children in whose house there was no trouble, who are fighting by proxies, capable of unleashing hostilities against any country, nuke hundreds of thousands as it was in Japan, or overthrow any government, neither considering state sovereignty nor a choice of citizens of any country, as soon as they see the interests of the United States and the permissible degree of risk.

So, you ask, where does the entire human being lost in them then? - The answer is simple: No one gives a name to the food. We do not think about the hard fate of the cow, considering beef on the counter. We only think about the quality of the product and its price. So, I suppose the Americans do not see specific people behind those who are going to kill or whose legitimately elected leader they intend to overthrow.

But no matter how much one tries to demand from the citizens of other countries to agree to the role of the cow, they will never agree to this, therefore, under the blow, Russia is forced to lead this struggle for the self-awareness and security of all countries in the world.

Our opponents have a chance to win only in one case - if they find the strength to adopt the tactics of the "enemy" - they will begin to tell the truth, listen to the opposite side, open their thoughts to their own people. The new administration of the White House still has a chance to start from scratch, writing off sins for its predecessors.

But how will they differ from their opponent then? How can one explain to his citizens what their insoluble contradictions with Russians are and what is their irreconcilable position? - And then there are two options. Either wars and conflicts will end, world defense spending will decrease, and trade will grow. Either these politicians will have to admit that they are ready to continue attacking other countries, not for good reasons, but solely for the sake of resources, maintaining their own fraudulent financial institutions or for unfair global competition.

But what kind of society will be able to reconcile with the second option, rejecting all the best and humane that we received from God, no matter what names we call him? "This is a question for historians studying the Third Reich, and I hope very much that we will not have a need for these historical analogies in the case of the Americans.

American-Kremlin trolls

My friend, an American journalist who is the founder of Our Russia, Phil Butler asked me a question about what I feel about his participation in this information war on the side of Russia. He knows the answer himself, but I think he wanted to hear it from me.

Our goodwill of citizens of the two countries is the beginning and the end of any discussions. As there will be no winners in the modern hot world war, there is a high chance that there will not be losers in the information war, and we work together, to ensure that the Cold War 2.0 is resolved in the interests of both nations, the world. To people of different nationalities and religions knew more about each other, and therefore did not fear each other and did not look for enemies where they do not exist. So that no one will be allowed to push each other to please someone's evil will.

I see him as an honest man, a friend and an interesting interlocutor who has chosen the side that allows him to be a journalist in the most primordial sense of the word - writing about what he knows, sees, and what he believes. He embodies what we believe in Russia, namely, that there are many people on the other side of the ocean who live by conscience and by God's laws, for whom humanism, honor and international law are not abstract concepts. Phil gives us an example of the responsible attitude to his destiny, because he offers his compatriots to think about the information that Western media feeding them, and to both sides to win this new media cold war so that it never progresses into a hot one.

Those who talk about the aggressive attitude of Russia and its alleged desire to restore the Soviet Union apparently do not know the map of the world. Russia is a huge country, with a relatively small population, enormous natural resources and a unique, strategic geographical location. As we say in a joke: "When we in Moscow set up the navigator to drive to Vladivostok, we hear:" After nine thousand kilometers turn to the right. "

We survived many wars that began with an attack on our territory and ended in the lair of the aggressor. We are always ready to repeat this experience, but the development of military technologies leaves less and less chance that there will be in winners such a war. For us, war is not an abstract concept, but a state of mind, a legacy of ancestors, which from the cradle prepares every citizen at a difficult time to protect his family, and the soil, and the country with weapons in their hands.

We are grateful to the Americans for the help they gave us in the Second World War, we honor the British heroes of the Northern convoys, and remember the docking of the Soyuz-Apollo spacecraft. We love the Private Ryan, Forest Gump, the Schindler list and the Lion King, and we sincerely do not understand why your politicians and the media are trying to make us enemies. We are insulted by their lies, that makes us feel threatened, to remember about Napoleon and Hitler, as well about a lot of other Western states that started aggression against Russia and the USSR and who ended bad. Let's talk more and teach each other so that no one could dictate to us that we should think about each other, and together we could make this world safer.

Stanislav Stankevich

In previous chapters I promised to discuss convergent strategies deployed by the globalists for the purpose of finally curtailing all opposing narratives. I decided that this section sarcastically titled "Blown", is the correct space for dealing with this false Russophobic narrative. It is also appropriate to address covert and overt strategies against Russia and those who would moderate here, because my friend Lt. Colonel Stankevich has firsthand knowledge of western intelligence communities operating in Russia's digital space. While the United States lawmakers and the Titans of the Internet technology space hammer out the eventual censoring of ideas over a measly $100,000 worth of Facebook ads, Israeli, US, and even European intelligence agencies and agents use Facebook and other platforms for spying with impunity[43].

The so called "Russiagate" affair after the election of Donald Trump has provided us with a mountain of evidence of desperate anti-Russia tactics in play. When the St. Petersburg troll story made famous by New York Times author Adrian Chen died out of the news cycle, we thought we'd seen the last of fantastical claims of troll armies[44]. But desperation and a new strategy to negate the pro-Russia social message saw

---

[43]*Beware! "Pokemons" in epaulets, or Where do fake heroes and impostors from special services come from?* (Осторожно! Покемоны» в погонах, или Откуда берутся лжегерои и самозванцы от спецслужб?), a report to the Interior Ministry of the Russian Federation, 2016

[44] *The Agency*, by Adrian Chen, New York Times, June 2, 2015

this narrative resuscitated. I believe that Donald Trump being elected was seen as a final proof positive that the globalist media was losing the war for the hearts and minds of digital society. Just a few weeks before the scheduled publication of this book, the key social media businesses were being leveraged for "proof" of Russia's interference in the U.S. elections. In a conspicuous sequence of announcements, first Facebook, then Twitter, and Google followed suit in implicating the Kremlin directly. Even though the public was given no evidence against the Putin administration, the government and business seem to be in collusion and bent on "pinning" the intrigue on Russian officials. In typical form United States officials seemed to act out a play scripted like the CNN news stories Trump admonished as "fake news" since he took office. Look at from a new media perspective, the amazing coincidences and scripted nature of these events are beyond suspicious. A clue that the senate investigation was a game strategy is revealed in a September story on CNN by author Jeremy Herb. In the story U.S. Senator Mark Warner warns constituents:

"Facebook's disclosure that it sold political ads to a Russian troll farm is just the "tip of the iceberg" when it came to election interference on social media."

As we see now, Warner obviously knew all too well the outcome of the strategy. As of October 20, 2017, Bloomberg and other mainstream media announced proposed laws to curtail first advertising in social media, and then free speech altogether. Bloomberg's Steven T. Dennis reported[45]:

"After months of congressional investigations into Russian interference with U.S. elections, legislation is gaining traction as senators introduced a bipartisan plan to impose new disclosure requirements for political ads on Facebook, Twitter, Google and other social media."

Now, emboldened by the public's apathy toward their own civil liberties, Senators propose a piece of legislation co-sponsored by the insane war hawk Senator John McCain, that proposes social platforms keep public "lists" of people who buy *election related ads* valued at more than $500. As innocuous and logical as this may sound, the law could be used as a kind of "kill list" for a political or ideological opposition. In essence, these senators are trying to skirt the U.S. Constitution in a move to retract certain liberties. A "for instance" here is my own activity as former owner of a small PR firm. Many smaller private entities in our business buy advertising for clients and for personal endeavors using Paypal and other means. I know that my own ad buys on Facebook in support for editorial about political subjects exceeds this $500 threshold. If this law is passed, Facebook and the others will "name" me and other private citizens "agents" of a kind. At least this will be so where geopolitical ideas are concerned. However, the overt and covert defensive measures the globalist cabal deploy converging

[45] *Senators Propose Social-Media Ad Rules After Months of Russia Probes*, by Steven T. Dennis, Bloomberg, October 19, 2017

government policy and business intelligence is only half the story. Offensive spying and anti-Russia spy games take place daily in social media. As I type this CNN helps create the new Red Scare using sensational headlines and the familiar "sources" and hearsay evidence to condemn Russia for a troll farm nobody has really proven exists[46]. This story has a familiar ring from the network caught admitting it bashes Russia to get more viewers and readers. In the piece the authors concoct an evil Russian oligarch tale involving businessman Yevgeny Prigozhin, a man Vladimir Putin's enemies say is his "chef." I am laughing as I read the Wikipedia reference to Prigozhin because even the voracity, facts, and neutrality of the article has already been questioned by Wikipedia authors since this "troll factory" aspect was added[47] back in April 2017. The article was created by a new Wikipedia author designated "Kap677-2", who joined on the March 6th, 2017 at 16:05 UTC, just hours before the article was created. This mystery Wikipedia editor also created the questionable Anti-Corruption Foundation reference, on the day he or she was welcomed to Wikipedia[48]. This article is about the NGO founded by none other than Putin hater Alex Nevalny. At least one sharp

---

[46] Exclusive: Putin's 'chef,' the man behind the troll factory, Tim Lister, Jim Sciutto and Mary Ilyushina, CNN, October 18, 2017

[47] *Yevgeny Prigozhin*, Wikipedia biography, new editor Kap677-2, March 7, 2017

[48] Anti-Corruption Foundation, Wikipedia article, contributed to by Kap677-2, March 7, 2017

Wikipedia editor questioned the new community member over possible connections to ACF, a fact which I also chuckled at because I am an editor at Wikipedia myself. For your reference, the conversation from the editor to this "Kap677-2" went like this:

> *"Hi, I'm UNSC Luke 1021. I went to the article Anti-Corruption Foundation, which you created. Reading through the article, I got the feeling that the main editor was related to the topic. I'm just wondering if you are closely connected to the article topic (the ACF), because I have to tag it as such. UNSC Luke 1021 (talk) 14:15, 28 March 2017 (UTC)"*

The reply was a simple "No, I am not AFC", which tells me Nevalny's minions were behind both questionable articles. As I've been forced to say before, these excavations are all ammunition for a future book. As a final note on this for now, this Kap677-2 person also ran into Wikipedia editor scrutiny when trying to edit another article entitled *"He Is Not Dimon to You"*, which is of course about the Russian documentary film by the Navalny people about alleged corruption by Prime Minister of Russia Dmitry Medvedev. This article, created by an anonymous Wikipedia user whose IP address leads to Odessa in Ukraine, shows the length and depth at which NATO and western intelligence operatives alongside Ukraine and Baltic nation extremists are embedded against Russia interests. Continuing for now, I must reflect on who the real social media aggressors are. The sources of CNN and U.S. Senate proofs are becoming more well-known without my interjection[4950]. Please see reports on U.S. State department spending more than $1.6 million for Voice of America and USAID on Facebook alone.

Discounting the millions of dollars spent by corporate or government controlled western media on social media platforms, efforts by western intelligence agencies and "so-called" NATO trolls dwarf the pitiful fairytale U.S. Senators and the technocrats have come up with. Since the end of this book was not intended to be about digital intelligence insurgents and Big Brother, I'll simply call the reader's attention to an effort by western intelligence that the Russians now lovingly refer to as *"Pokemons in epaulets"*. It turns out, my FSB colleague Stanislav Stanislavic has been on the trail of infiltrators, spies, and saboteurs of the Russia message on social media for some time now. Stanislavic's role in Alpha Team was focused on new digital intelligence and even countermeasures, if I recall correctly. So, once the over the top social media investigations began in September and accelerated in October, I asked Stanislav (Stas) for any information at all on the alleged St. Petersburg troll factory, the Internet Research Agency, and anything else pertinent to the mudslinging effort from the west. As fate would have it, the former FSB colonel had just completed an investigation

---

[49] *US government agencies are buying ads on Facebook—in Russian*, by Hanna Kozlowska, Quartz, October 13, 2017

[50] *It's not just Moscow: American agencies use Facebook to woo Russians*, too, by Carl Prine, The San Diego Union-Tribune, October 13, 2017

into western intelligence services and so-called "NATO trolls" creating bogus identities on Facebook for the purpose of intelligence gathering and sewing discontent in Russia, and etc. According to a document Stanislav shared with me entitled *"Pokemons: Fake Secret/Special Service Men"* (ПОКЕМОНЫ: САМОЗВАНЦЫ «ОТ СПЕЦСЛУЖБ) details the investigation by former Alpha Team members into the true identities of imposters. The was an investigation by the organization of veterans of the FSB's Team Alpha, was shared in interviews in October of 2017 with the Ministry of the Interior of the Russian Federation concerned about the "Pokemon" issue.

Once again, I am forced to leave off deeper revelations here. This Alice in Wonderland rabbit hole is deep and expansive. As a last discovery here, I know it will not surprise most readers to know that the source of the "breaking" CNN story on the financier of the alleged "troll factory" is none other than CNN's and CNBC's Russian partner RBC TV, the business news channel formerly run by Yelizaveta Osetinskaya, who joins Alex Navalny and others as top Putin haters. And the hole does not lead to many reputable western media entities, I will assure you. A Business Inside piece with the stunning title *"Our task was to set Americans against their own government': New details emerge about Russia's trolling operation"* links to and cites these unfounded stories as if they were religious icons. Even a shallow investigation into facts refutes nearly everything the U.S. Senate has in front of it. At least concerning "who" bankrolled an imaginary troll farm bent on disrupting America[51].

Summing up here we find a multitude of facts, logic, and probability pointing to a rather simple explanation for recent moves by U.S. lawmakers, technocrat business interests, and their media partners against Putin and Russia. If I were CNN, I would put the story to readers like this. *"Exclusive: Globalists tied to failed Russian oligarchs make our laws"*, or something to this effect. A CNN story of this type would probably link Alex Nevalny with ousted oligarch and alleged Russian mafioso Mikhail Khodorkovsky, who would in turn be linked to Rothschild banking interests that failed in Russia because of Putin. Subsequent stories might "reveal" further ties in between Alex Nevalny and CNN affiliates, imaginary NATO farms run and funded by CIA operatives, as well as hearsay evident and supposition pointing to U.S. politicians and the deep state colluding with money interests that control these media resources. A story of this kind, should a journalist or publisher like me decide to fabricate it, would then be disseminated across a massive network of desperate and/or broken publications/networks worldwide. Without so much as a scrap of paper proving Senator John McCain (for instance) has connections to the Mafia (let's say) a false narrative (or fake news) could in fact become an alternative truth for hundreds of millions of people. As was the case with

---

[51] *'Our task was to set Americans against their own government': New details emerge about Russia's trolling operation,* by Sonam Sheth, Business Insider, October 17, 2017

the highly publicized "Panama Papers", the research for which was shown to have been funded by George Soros, this Putin election meddling fairytale hasn't an inkling of proof. Nothing ties Vladimir Putin to the offshore tax evasion schemes of the real mafiosos, and nothing ties Putin or the Kremlin to a puny Facebook ad budget. My own efforts at promoting editorial and analysis by me on Facebook, probably exceed the Kremlin's expenditures. The reality is simple, everybody promotes on Facebook, and Russiagate is hyperbole, as can be seen in stacks of reports and independent news stories[52]. As author Aaron Maté points out in the cited The Nation article, "the media has substituted hype for evidence". More significantly, it appears U.S. lawmakers have also substituted desired policy for truth.

If only Putin's troll army had the resources and reach the opposition does! But more on that in my final confession.

[52] *Russiagate Is More Fiction Than Fact*, by Aaron Mate, The Nation, October 7, 2017

Chapter XIV: The Last Confession

"We know that our governments lie. We know that our media channels lie. We search for integrity and truth among the rubble of propaganda. We want to pin our hopes on power for good."
Vanessa Beeley

Now I am sure "my cover is blown." I confess to having connections with some of Russia's most loyal citizens in high and common positions. In just over three years I've been befriended by the producers of Russia's most popular TV shows, by photographers and writers, by artists and ballet legends, local and federal politicians, Olympic athletes, and even Spetsnaz officers. This happenstance was not because of any special character of mine, not because any money changed hands, and especially not because Vladimir Putin sent me out from the Kremlin to engage in his anti-NATO propaganda. The ordinary and extraordinary Russians befriended me and some of these others because we defended them – period. As difficult as this may be for some to imagine, the hand of friendship goes a very, very long way in Mother Russia.

So far, I have presented many of the most well-known pro-Russian influencers in the digital world. They have contributed in their own words, their motivations, ideas, and ideals concerning the clearly anti-Russia propaganda war that has raged the last three or four years. I've also attempted to explain my own motivations and role in all this, which turns out to be a mirror of my colleagues' involvement. The noted international correspondent, Pepe Escobar introduced the book and the prevailing "Putin troll" sentiment you've read over-and-over again. The Saker, Charles Bausman, Graham Phillips, and Vanessa Beeley showed you the broad and sweeping independent media path of truth, and on the dissenting view on Russia. And the real Kremlin heroes, if I may, they showed you the crisp reality of this war on Russia and Russians – and this is common decency heated to a raging boil.

People like Eric Anderson down on the Amazon, artist Carmen Renieri, and disabled veterans like Paul Payer, they show us all the real power behind Vladimir Putin, the wisdom, and strength of truth. Facing the biggest lie in the history of humanity dead in the face, decent people of every nationality just said, "Wait one damn minute!" Ordinary people, people watching their grandkids, people in wheelchairs, old soldiers on breathing machines, bloggers and stock market speculators, teachers, lawyers, adventurers, and stay at home moms got tired of unsportsmanlike conduct – there is nothing more to it. This book has shown this irrevocably for anyone with an ounce of moderation and decency in their soul. The simple truth is, there are paid journalists like Pepe Escobar, Robert Parry, scholars like

Stephen Cohen, and experts like Dr. Paul Craig Roberts in the mix for moderation on Russia. I confess my admiration for them all, for their courage in the face of overwhelming dangers.

As for the opposing force, I can tell you as a former editor of several highly influential media sources, these "forces" of which I speak are as devastating as they are diabolical. There's yet another subject for a book, but the point of these people and their brave efforts should be well made. To cement the dangerous nature of this force a story in the New Yorker[53] by Internet culture expert Adrian Chen contains a warning from the opposing technocracy side of all this. In the report Chen wrote:

> "Bogus news stories, which overwhelmingly favored Trump, did flood social media throughout the campaign, and the hack of the Clinton campaign chair John Podesta's e-mail seems likely to have been the work of Russian intelligence services. But, as harmful as these phenomena might be, the prospect of legitimate dissenting voices being labelled fake news or Russian propaganda by mysterious groups of ex-government employees, with the help of a national newspaper, is even scarier."

---

[53] *The Propaganda About Russian Propaganda*, by Adrian Chen, The New Yorker, December 1, 2016

The people who are the opponents of "Kremlin Trolls" are an imposing force. Journalists and experts spouting Russia hate are well funded, well educated, and work under an almost impenitrable dome of protection created by government, coprorate interests, banking interests, and the trillions of dollars supra-capitalism runs off the printing presses of central banks. The evangelists of NATO and the globalists, the minions of the insane Russophobes, they sop up the drippings from the tables of business giants and elite bankers whose names we are all familiar with by now. I've mentioned George Soros, USAID, the CIA, NATO and its own trolls, the United States State Department, the governments of the United Kingdom and of the EU, corporate media such as Bertelsmann and Axel Springer, the IMF and other financial organizations, and hundreds of NGOs, all of which played a huge role in this ongoing media war. The vastness of the effort to discredit and dishonor Vladimir Putin and Russia is almost unimaginable.

Not until Donald Trump was elected president did I even realize just how desperate and deadly the globalist elite had become. Imagine how Soros and his colleagues in London or Luxembourg must feel, having paid untold trillions to create a new liberal world order, only to be thwarted by a few crazy journalists, some drunken writers, a few aging grandmas, a platoon of marginalized old soldiers, and a pissed off travel agent or two. Pitiful is the only word that describes the nasty and wasteful movement against the Russians in all this. It's pitiful for whole industries and world organizations to fail so miserably in subduing an opposing message – our message of opposition. Think about it for a moment, the billionaires and bankers, the politicians and bureaus, the untold thousands of paid pundits against Vladimir Putin. Then imagine if you can a ragtag gang of rusty conquistadors like me and these others beating them into a frenzy. Gasp the enormity of Russian media like RT and Sputnik, with their pitiful budgets in rubles, striking utter fear into the heart of the globalist beast. Aided and abetted by this old technology blogger turned politico, and by a couple of hundred more zealots who are disenchanted by the false American Dream, a tiny group of virtual "nobodies" drove the Germans to create a "Truth Ministry", the EU to pass "anti-propaganda" legislation, and America's ruling class and technocrats to scream "foul" through their media machine. Yes, Kremlin Troll voices became the New World Order's worst nightmare.

> *"Throughout history, it has been the inaction*
> *of those who could have acted; the*
> *indifference of those who should have*
> *known better; the silence of the voice of*
> *justice when it mattered most; that has*
> *made it possible for evil to triumph."*
> ### Haile Selassie

The entities arrayed against any positive message about Russia have no plausible deniability for the disparate roles they've played in all this chaos. There's no need for me to provide further proof of my own government's role than the

National Defense Authorization Act, signed into effect by outgoing President Barack Obama, which included a $160 million revamping of the "Global Engagement Center" to combat Russian propaganda. An article via The Nation by Adam H. Johnson[54] framed the most pertinent aspects of this center so:

> "When asked by The Nation if the State Department was targeting Americans or paying American journalists, State Department spokesperson Nicole Thompson wouldn't say they weren't, only that, "the Global Engagement Center targets its messaging at foreign audiences abroad."

Of special importance here, is a section of the bill signed by Obama that points to the US government funding journalism and journalists arrayed against the Russia message. The Nation article cited this section:

> "The legislation establishes a fund to help train local journalists and provide grants and contracts to NGOs, civil society organizations, think tanks, private sector companies, media organizations, and other experts outside the U.S. government with experience in identifying and

---

[54] *US Officials Won't Say if a New Anti–Russia Propaganda Project Is Targeting Americans,* by Adam H. Johnson, The Nation, March 9, 2017

*analyzing the latest trends in foreign
government disinformation techniques."*

In no uncertain terms, the $160 million earmarked by the Obama decree could be used to fund characters like Bellingcat, Weisburd, Soros NGOs, or even companies set up with the explicit purpose of defeating "guess who?" Yes, those of us labeled Kremlin or Putin trolls by the real trolls in this information war. The powers that control the monstrosity that has become western business-government have not learned a lesson by being beaten to pieces by unpaid amateurs and truth seekers, they've decided to throw still more money at their problem just like they did in funding the Russia-focused, English-language *Interpreter* magazine, which allegedly funded not only by the US State Department but by the family of ousted Russian oligarch and mafioso, Mikhail Khodorkovsky. The magazine is led by the aforementioned Daily Beast editor, Michael Weiss is a prime example of the new western oligarchy propaganda. Weiss, who is another prototypical "agent" of the neocon narrative, *headed up a neocon PR project known as "Just Journalism,"* which policed (trolled) the English-language press for any journalism critical of Israel in the wake of its brutal war on Gaza of 2008 and 2009[55]. Weiss has provoked much criticism from journalists and experts who live outside the corporate

---

[55] Hysterical beast: The problem with The Daily Beast's Russia analysis, RT Op-Edge, October 8, 2015

or governmental budgetary matrix. Another scathing report[56] by James Carden entitled "Neo-McCarthyism and the US Media," betrays the clear mission against any semblance of moderate thought about Russia. Here is Carden on the relationship of Weiss and other western journalists to the anti-Russia narrative:

> "Weiss and Pomerantsev (Peter) have joined the long line of Western journalists who have played to the public's darkest suspicions about the power, intentions and reach of those governments that are perceived as threats to the United States. In his seminal essay on McCarthyism, "The Paranoid Style in American Politics," the historian Richard Hofstadter wrote that in the worldview of these opportunists, "very often the enemy is held to possess some especially effective source of power: he controls the press; he has unlimited funds; he has a new secret for influencing the mind (brainwashing)." There exists no better précis of Weiss and Pomerantsev's view of Putin and the Russian government's media apparatus."

The list of western journalists, analysts, professors, bureaucrats, military figures, bankers, and politicians who've thrown in on the bashing of Putin and Russia is longer than both my arms and legs. I cannot begin to even list them, and especially not their roles here. The sheer numerical superiority these globalist pundits maintain dwarfs and muster of alleged Kremlin trolls.

---

[56] *Neo-McCarthyism and the US Media*, by James Carden, The Nation, May 19, 2015

This brings me to the final confessional of the book – my own. But first let me say that I really admired how Pepe Escobar handled the introduction to this book. Though we've never been close friends, he answered my request to contribute to the book like a true comrade and caring pal. The "piss off" ending was as close to perfect as I can imagine. Somehow though, just telling the denizens of Russophobic darkness to "stick it," it just does not say it all for me. So, let me be clear on my message in writing this book.

First and foremost, I decided that someone should chronicle the real people that stood up to one of the most powerful propaganda narratives ever leveled onto humanity. The idea that Putin and Russia have been in anything but defense mode these last years, it is preposterous. The only reason anybody on the globe even considers Putin or Russia as aggressors is due solely to the humongous investments and resources that power the anti-Russia message. Many decent people, and especially those mentioned herein, could not stand by and see this lie accepted. I believe I have helped to show this in the book you just read. In my way, I hope I have added a footnote to history, a footnote that acknowledges the extraordinary people who defeated an omnipotent and stoic, ultimately evil media empire. If the 300 Spartans are looking down observing what unbelievable odds are these days, then "Kremlin Trolls" are modern heroes. This facet paves the path for my final confession – my utter and ghastly hatred for the purveyors of humanity's suffering.

These purveyors of humankind's suffering are tyrannical on a global scale. My utter contempt for them comes from my father and his father, and from the decent human beings I've known all my life. America and Americans were supposed to stand up for righteousness and truth, at least according to my father and his peers. But the same people setting fire to the world today, and their institutions, are the same ones that murdered the millions since before the modern age. My personal contempt for each of them and my deep desire that they fail in every endeavor, lies in the hope and the prayer that justice might prevail. So here is my message to them.

If I were a George Soros, or a Rothschild banker, a Rockefeller clone, or some German industrialist son of an escaped Nazi war criminal, I'd be appalled at the utter inefficiency and uselessness my money had wrought. If a trillion dollars or more could not buy me absolute media control, if thousands of paid journalists, professors, activists, CEOs, bureaucrats, judges, and movie stars could not secure my omnipotence against RT television and the walking wounded of the world, I'd fire every single, solitary henchman I'd employed. You failed my dear sirs, and you failed miserably. All your machinations, money, and mind-boggling skullduggery against one man supported only by a relative few. Why, Vladimir Putin, with one ten thousandths of your media, corporate, and organizational resources, he bashed you to smithereens these last few years. You are pitiful.

Absolutely horrid were your efforts. Not only have your economics, and your pseudo-democracies failed, but you cannot even hire decent rats to row your ships of fools. Your names really do not matter. Whether you are Jeff Bezos types, technocrats who think buying the news puts you above the law of man, or even if you are super cool billionaires like Sir Richard Branson, hanging with former presidents, the stain of mediocrity and failure is upon you, just the same. Like every other group of two-bit tyrants that ever lived, you've underestimated the little people, but there's more.

It is so difficult to describe the basal and personal level at which I and others have taken all these machinations for ruling the world we live in. I guess I am like most of the others if they'd have just played a bit fairly at Sochi. Or if only we never knew about the new Ukraine Nazis controlling Odessa with an iron fist. Maybe if at least some of the bombs and artillery shells had fallen outside the Donbass or Gaza, or Yemen, if the NSA and the president had never lied, then just maybe me and others like me could have stomached their Orwellian rule over us all. But we did watch and see an American president shame us before the world, only to call it "exceptionalism." So, this is why I hope the opposition takes my book and my message deeply personally, just like I've taken all their evil bullshit the last four years. And you wonder why so many admire Vladimir Putin?

The obviousness of excellence amid mediocrity is the reason.

Watching Vladimir Putin operate among today's amoral misfit leaders is like seeing Usain Bolt running against a mannequin, or an eagle flying above a penguin. The most powerful leader in the last half century, Putin never hesitates to walk alongside his people, as in his participation with the Immortal Regiment at Moscow's May 9th ceremonies in memory of the Great Patriotic War. He's also widely admired for being dignified when other world leaders act up in a juvenile manner at solemn occasions. When American or French leaders have their aids hold umbrellas over their heads, Putin lays wreaths before slain heroes standing stoically alone beneath the storm like a real man – solemn in his respectfulness and correctness[57]. While his detractors proclaim such "Putin moments" are contrived photo ops, the man is seen as genuine by the people. It took me quite a bit of time to find the idea that might crystalize the essence of all the people mentioned in this book, but I finally did find it in a passage from the Japanese culture. The idea also conveys how many people feel about Vladimir Putin.

> *"Bushido as an independent code of ethics may*
> *vanish, but its power will not perish from the*
> *earth; its schools of martial prowess or civic*
> *honor may be demolished, but its light and its*

---

[57] *Putin stands in the rain in front of honour guards during a wreath-laying ceremony marking the anniversary of the Nazi German invasion in 1941,* Pictures of the Day, the Telegraph, June 23, 2017

glory will long survive their ruins. Like its symbolic flower, after it is blown to the four winds, it will still bless mankind with the perfume with which it will enrich life."
Inazo Nitobe - *Bushido: The Soul of Japan*

I've studied Putin as much as anyone has these last three years and I can tell you honestly, he identifies with both the martial prowess and the blessings honor bestows. Vladimir Putin finds favor by something carried on the wind, something no one can really describe. Perhaps this is why the ne'er-do-well seem to hate him so much. Human beings have always held out hope in leadership. It is spiritual mostly, the way we cling to the hierarchical way – God, family, and country – this is who we shall always be. So, understanding how Putin never seems to lose to the globalists becomes easy when one considers his defending of Russia against the onslaught of the opportunists who want to tear her apart.

Finally, for those who have disgraced and dishonored us with lies, war, waste, and crisis there is but one elegant reprieve. I leave this gift offering for them. May the unjust and those who trod heavily on us, who killed, us, and who were disdainful of all honor, here is your emancipation. If you have one ounce of decency and courage from your forebears, you'll take this opportunity to salvage honor. A single bullet is dreadful cheap after all you've wasted.

Afterword

It's 5:35 a.m. on October 19th, 2017. It's less than a week until Red October, and the day I announced I would publish *Putin's Praetorians*. In the runup, I thought everything except for this introduction to RT's Editor-In-Chief Margarita Simonyan's contribution was done. But the last three weeks have been explosive about media and policymaker attacks on Russia, Russian sympathizers, and on independent media overall. Some ads bought on Facebook by a Russian social influence outfit, a U.S. Senate witch hunt, and the government/financial cabal that runs America are threatening to either shut down, censor, and label RT America, or to out-and-out criminalize anyone and anything associated. So, I am compelled to go one step further with my introduction of Russia's top media personality. At the beginning of this book, I quoted Robert Lewis Stevenson: *"The world has no room for cowards."* So, if I were to keep separate and impersonal any relationship I have in Russia, this story will not be a kosher confessional. Here is briefly what I know of the person most responsible for a media miracle RT became and of the attempts to hide, obscure, and destroy the other side of the story forever.

Westerners who might have heard the name Margarita Simonyan regarding her being the propaganda mistress for the archvillain Vladimir Putin are wildly misled. Few who believe such tales ever take the time to learn about her early life. Hardly anyone in America knows of her study there, and especially not of her ideas about Americans. I am sure it will surprise most people reading this to learn about her keen intellect and her moderate view on America and Russia. While I admit having no original intention of profiling Margarita here, I was compelled by the current negatively charged media atmosphere. From the time the young journalist took the reins of the fledgling RT network, the dominant theme was the effort to tell the other side of the story on Russia and other topics. A narrative from Washington back in 2008 reflects my contentions about Simonyan better and in a more unbiased manner than I ever could. Reading the article for this last section, I could not help smiling at some of Simonyan's comments[58]. At the time, Simonyan told author Karen Rowland about how the war in Chechnya demanded the Russia side of things be related. On the mission of RT in the wake of the Beslan school incident which saw 186 children killed, Simonyan commented:

> *"The purpose is mainly to tell the world about Russia, what sort of country we are, why what's happening is happening, to explain things that might not be so obvious and also to give an alternative view of the world."*

---

[58] *Russia Today: Youth served*, by Kara Rowland, The Washington Times, October 27, 2008

RT's boss goes on in the article to explain how the "stereotypical" Russia personality has been formed by the western media, and subsequently by the media consumer. Back then, she pointed to the ease with which media and the public perceive the new Russia just like the old Soviet Union. And looking at the situation today we see these perceptions used to devastating effect, while Simonyan is continually forced to defend the viability of this "other" narrative. As one of the main ones seeking to defend both free thinking and the role of the opposition view, I'm often called a "Kremlin apologist" for merely stating the obvious. This brings me to the point of introducing the Margarita Simonyan who I know. I've thought a great deal about how to help readers understand the real honesty and professionalism of this journalist, without expressing myself in an unemotional way – and I decided this is impossible. So, here's what I can tell you from the heart.

When RTTV called me in Germany February 7th, 2014, the same day the opening ceremonies of the Sochi Olympics were scheduled to begin, I confess I was stunned. Then, when a CBC TV colleague called after the live show to quip, *"Phil, what the hell was that? Nobody gets 5 consecutive uninterrupted minutes on the air like that,"* I got more and more interested in how RT worked. Looking back now, I realize it was probably Margarita herself that arranged the programming for that day in Sochi. Today, I am grateful for my own decision to keep a respectful distance from somebody I would otherwise have sought closer ties with. You see, I take a certain pride in my ability to meet just about anybody. And in my job as a PR executive, this has proved to be advantageous many times. I like people, and they like me. Getting access and communicating with the advisers of former President Barack Obama (see volume two next year), with the world's biggest PR names, with sports figures and movie personalities, and especially with politicians – it's just natural and fun for me. In the case of Margarita Simonyan, I chose to keep a respectful distance. The reason for this was not simply out of esteem though. To be honest, I somehow suspected that intelligence agencies, combative media, the "so-called" NATO trolls, and a host of adversaries might later have a field day if there were any one-to-one relationships. For the same reason, I refused any payment for writing editorials, I felt it was necessary to maintain a sort of professional distance. However, this "distance" never prevented me from knowing exactly who she was. If you were the NSA using Gmail to record all my communications with Russia, you would see clearly my methodology for "knowing" the people I deal with. As somebody in the business of words, I expect profiling writers is something RT's boss knows as well as I do. That said, the authority of unspoken communication used to support helpless little kids is something that binds people together even more than philosophies or ideals. Simonyan's humanity outside the limelight allows me to attest to her character. Also, if one is caring enough to observe, a harried look of weariness or a LiveJournal opinion that shows her passion for the network she almost single-handedly created is revealing. I could go on about Margarita's charitable endeavors or about how she is a near perfect reflection of the intelligence, wit, humor, and humanity of Putin himself. Haven't you noticed that all those closest to Russia's president mirror the same smart and capable aura? To return to my special relationship with such people, I've found that the biggest test of character, in the end, is trust. For instance, Margarita trusted me to say what was in my heart and in my character when it counted most for Russia and for RT at Sochi. And I trusted my intelligence, instinct and inner voice enough all along so that I might be able to see the real Margarita Simonyan, the real Vladimir Putin, and the real Russia behind the stereotype shown me my entire life by the American establishment.

Margarita Simonyan is one of those people who you feel privileged to call a friend, and one your ashamed to ask for a favor of for knowing how many she supports. And as sometimes happens, she's the type that when you finally hazard a request, she delivers more than you expected. Now I leave you to ponder why Vladimir Putin chose this woman to create something compelling and amazing for Russia and the people of the world.

Reflecting on the Outward Voice of Russia

by Margarita Simonyan

For a very long time we had the same few outlets setting the news narrative about the entire world, for the entire world. They had the same people telling the same stories, often casting aside important issues and voices. But we know that the world is more diverse, more complicated than that, and that people across the globe have been hungry, for a long time, for a news source that truly reflects this diversity of stories and opinions. This is the 'why' and the 'how' of RT finding its space in a crowded news universe: by reporting on what the mainstream media ignores.

Our goal has never been to diminish anything or anyone else. Our mission isn't to shout down other news sources – including those we consider 'mainstream media'. Yet we do aspire to providing greater diversity in news at large, to serve the audiences by helping them break out of the mainstream media echo chamber. And yes, it is an echo-chamber. We have seen it time and time again: whatever internal politics may be a cause of disagreements between news outlets within any given country, whenever larger international stories become involved, most of these outlets sing in unison. There are predetermined good guys and bad guys, and the narrative becomes almost identical for nearly every paper and TV channel.

In Russia, there are a lot of media outlets that openly support the US and the West in their anti-Russian sanctions, many journalists who openly go on Russian TV to voice their support for any anti-Russian acts or restrictions, and even media organizations that openly oppose the Kremlin's entire foreign policy. It's a precedent unimaginable in, for example, the US news media – to see people supporting anti-American sanctions imposed by another country, or supporting a US adversary. In Russia it happens all the time.

Or take the presidential election in France. From the start, there was a clear media darling – Emmanuel Macron. He was by far the front-cover fix on most, if not all, newspapers and magazines. Perhaps there was some critical coverage of Mr. Macron when it came to internal debates. But when his team made entirely baseless statements that RT was spreading "fake news" about Macron, not a single major French newspaper or TV channel even bothered to ask for a sole example of the supposed transgression. Nor did they check RT content for any of these supposed "fake news" items. Of course, they wouldn't have found any, if they did. And yet, French media outlets simply reprinted these libelous statements without question or scrutiny. Nobody challenged the establishment narrative. This isn't something simply lamentable. Myopia in news and public discourse can be downright dangerous.

Instead of aiding in dialogue and mutual understanding, this news media is broadening the understanding gap and escalating tensions. Which is why alternative voices – on any story, any issue – are critical to a healthy public debate. Today, more than ever before.

Margarita Simonyan

Editor-On-Chief, RT

About the Author

Phil Butler is a digital, media, and geopolitical analyst, who was first influential in the Web technology space. After joining a prominent digital public relations firm in Germany, Pamil Visions PR, he became an influential voice in internet media relations.

As a digital analyst and futurist, Butler examined new strategies and advised major web-based companies on leveraging online traditional and social media. His work during this time enabled technology startup companies to achieve success in a highly competitive market, providing forward-looking marketing services that promoted them to better understand the digital media landscape. As a result of his work in this field, Butler helped develop some of the most successful digital PR and marketing strategies in the field.

At the onset of the new "media war" in between the United States-EU actors and Russia, Butler served as an analyst to help independent media better understand the tools being arrayed against Russia and all opponents to the globalist narrative. A sought-after media analyst and speaker, Butler has been a guest on RTTV, Russia One TV, NTV Russia, and a cited authority by dozens of other major independent media outlets worldwide.

He now lives on the Island of Crete in Greece with his wife Mihaela, and their young son Paul-Jules.

Acknowledgements

I would like to take this opportunity to acknowledge and thank the people who helped make telling this story possible. To the "Kremlin Trolls" I failed to frame here, and to those who must go unnamed, the world does truly owe a great debt. Were it not for the extraordinary diligence and consideration of these people, one of the greatest injustices ever suffered by humanity might not have been revealed. The fact that a very few rather ordinary people stood against the most powerful business, political, and media forces in history is epic in and of itself.

Thanks to a wonderful Russian lady whose name cannot be shared for fear of peer pressures from neighbors in southern California, the dissenting view on V.V. Putin took hold in social media more fervently. Were in not for an unnamed couple whose relatives live in Ukraine, the globalist narrative would surely have dominated in the professional and entertainment circles. People like these, with family still in devastated place of crisis, cannot be cited for the genuine danger of recriminations. And the journalists who've adopted pen-names in order to protect their jobs and families, they shall remain anonymous until the day comes when truth is not a liability.

Then there are the inspirational influencers I need to thank, for while they are not "Kremlin Trolls" in the perfect sense, they synthesized or amplified the alternative view on Putin, Russia, and the globalist cabal. People like award winning journalists Robert Parry, linguist and philosopher Noam Chomsky, economist Paul Craig Roberts, Princeton Professor Stephen F. Cohen, and Professor Michel Chossudovsky have all made an indelible mark on this moment in human history. These great minds, along with a score of other deep thinkers and researchers, they provided the much-needed authority required to rescue the truth for human kind.

I'd also like the acknowledge journalists involved for RT, Sputnik, and other independent media. Authors and TV journalists like RT's *In the Now* analyst Anissa Naouai are owed an incalculable debt. Former RT *Breaking the Set* host Abby Martin became household names for their gripping and revealing programs calling to question western mainstream narratives, and she still champions causes like that of the embattled Palestinians dehumanized in Isreal. Other names that became famous for voicing moderation or outright dissent were Andrew Korybko of Sputnik, Neil Clark for RT and Sputnik, and Finian Cunningham, who often took hard knocks for being Kremlin Trolls. The truth of the matter on these writers is, they're either doing the job or serving up their research and views as honest journalists. RT's Max Keiser, Peter Lavelle who launched the much read The Duran, and Robert Bridge also fall into this category. While some journalists like Mark Sleboda and even the indubitable Tyler Durden of Zero Hedge wore the *Kremlin Troll badge* a time or two, they were professional analysts in other spheres long before this new media war heated up. The same is true for one of the most important voices of anti-globalist doctrine, award winning author F. William Engdahl, who's a colleague also contributing to New Eastern Outlook. Some will recall Engdahl as a well cited investigative journalist far back into the 1970's, and he published "*A Century of War: Anglo-American Oil Politics and the New World Order*" back in 2004. I'd be remiss if I did not mention Veterans Today Managing Editor Jim Dean and the indomitable Gordon Duff, who have been tireless in their efforts to provide thought provoking reports and deep intelligence regarding the *deep state*[59] and the clandestine network underneath what the public perceives.

Of course, there are many other "so-called" pro-Russia sympathizers I cannot mention for previously specified reasons. There are also a few I simply am forgetting to mention or who have asked to be omitted for other reasons. There's also several dozens of independent media outlets that without their publishing of these dissenting views, the world would simply have no clue as to any alternative Russia news. A couple that come to mind are 21st Century Wire, Fort Russ, and Moon of Alabama. To these publishers and well-wishers, we all owe a great debt of gratitude. And finally, these "top" Kremlin Trolls I've captured for you would have absolutely zero influence were it not for the millions of people who read their articles, retweet their tweets, share

---

[59] *What Is the Deep State*, by Greg Gandin, the Nation, February 17, 2017

their Facebook posts, and who watch their TV or YouTube broadcasts. While these adversaries to the globalist media are very few by comparison to their western mainstream counterparts, their efforts will thankfully never go unnoticed. Their passion for telling the truth nobody wanted to hear will always be remembered.

Made in the USA
San Bernardino, CA
28 November 2017